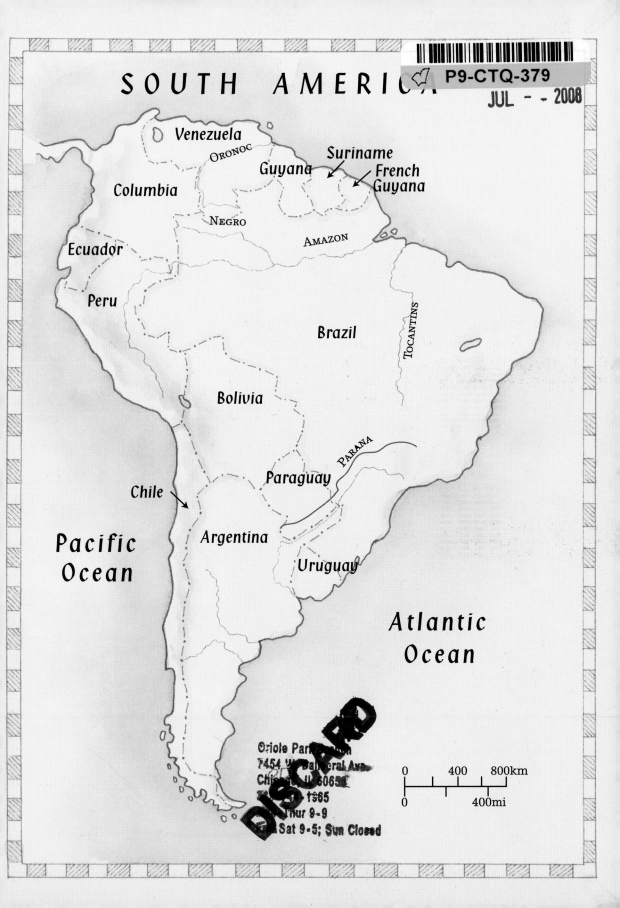

SOUTH AMERICA

Venezuela

ORONOC

Columbia

Suriname

Guyana

French Guyana

NEGRO

AMAZON

Ecuador

Peru

Brazil

TOCANTINS

Bolivia

PARANA

Chile

Paraguay

Argentina

Pacific Ocean

Uruguay

Atlantic Ocean

| 0 | 400 | 800km |

| 0 | | 400mi |

Holy Friends

Thirty Saints and Blesseds
of the Americas

Written by Diana M. Amadeo

Illustrated by Irina Lombardo
with Augusta Curreli

Pauline
BOOKS & MEDIA
Boston

Library of Congress Cataloging-in-Publication Data

Amadeo, Diana M.
   Holy friends : thirty saints and blesseds of the Americas / written by Diana
M. Amadeo ; illustrated by Irina Lombardo with Augusta Curreli.
         p. cm.
   Includes index.
   ISBN 0-8198-3384-3 (hardcover)
   1. Christian saints—Biography—Juvenile literature. 2. Christian biogra-
phy—Juvenile literature. I. Lombardo, Irina. II. Curreli, Augusta. III. Title.
   BR1711.A45 2005
   282'.092'27—dc22

                              2005002964

Map Illustrations by Sophie Kittredge

Published by Pauline Books & Media, 50 Saint Pauls Avenue, Boston, MA
02130-3491.

Printed in Korea

www.pauline.org

Pauline Books & Media is the publishing house of the Daughters of St. Paul,
an international congregation of women religious serving the Church with the
communications media.

1 2 3 4 5 6 7 8 9   11 10 09 08 07 06 05

This book is dedicated to my Lord,

through whom all things are possible.

To my parents, Jo and Jerome Schmitt,

who shared their love and belief in God.

And to my family: my husband Len,

and my children Angelique, Antony, and Desiree.

You have given my life purpose,

joy and insight. I love you all.

Contents

United States of America

Acknowledgments

This book would not have been possible without the groundwork of healing, spiritual support, and direction from Reverend Thomas Duston; Reverend Michael Sevigny, OFM CAP; Reverend Siluvai R. Selvappan "Father Cross"; Reverend Leo LeBlanc; Reverend Ralph DiOrio; Sr. Doris Gagnon, PM; Sr. Mary Joseph, APB; Sr. Lucille Blais, CSC; Sr. Patricia Edward Jablonski, FSP; Sr. Donna Giaimo, FSP; and Diane Lynch. And to my special Secular Franciscan family: thank you for reminding me to live the Gospel. *Pax et bonum.*

Blessed Laura Vicuña

1891–1904

"Oh my God, I give you my soul, my heart, my whole self."

Laura Vicuña was born in Santiago, Chile, in 1891. Her father, Joseph Vicuña, was a soldier, and her mother, Mercedes, was the daughter of a farmer. Soon after Laura's birth, civil war broke out in Chile. The Vicuñas fled from Santiago and went to live in Temuco, where life was safer. When Laura was two years old, her sister, Julia, was born. Soon after Julia's birth, Señor Vicuña died.

Señora Vicuña stayed with her daughters in Temuco until Laura was eight. She ran a store, but life was very hard, and the family was poor. Hoping to find a better job, Señora Vicuña took her children to Argentina. When they arrived, she was unable to find a job. She met a wealthy man named Manuel Mora, who persuaded her to come live with him at his *hacienda,* or ranch.

Señora Vicuña knew it would be sinful to live with Señor Mora when they were not married, but she agreed to do it. In return, Señor Mora promised her money and protection. He was not a good man. He treated her very badly, and sometimes even beat her.

Señora Vicuña wanted her daughters to be safe. She sent them to a boarding school run by the Daughters of Mary, Help of Christians, also known as the Salesian Sisters. Laura was nine years old. She worried about her mother, who would be left alone with Señor Mora. She prayed that her mother would leave the *hacienda*.

Laura loved the sisters and her life at the boarding school. When new girls came to school, Laura made them feel welcome. She always shared what she had with the poor children of the town. Laura made her First Communion when she was ten. She also joined the Sodality of the Children of Mary. The young girl developed a deep love for Jesus and Mary, and prayed often in the chapel before the Blessed Sacrament.

In 1902, Laura was visiting the *hacienda* over holiday break. One day, Señor Mora began trying to hurt her. Laura was very frightened. She ran outside to get away from him. She begged God to help her and to save her mother from this life of fear and sin. Each night she prayed, "Lord, I give you my life of loving service and sacrifice. Please help save my mother."

December of 1903 was cold, rainy, and damp. At school, Laura was very ill. With each passing day, she grew weaker. Her mother rented rooms near the school and came to care for her daughter. But Laura was not getting better.

In January, a drunken Señor Mora came to the rooms. "I'll stay here tonight," he announced. Laura's mother tried to reason with him, but he insisted. Laura, although very weak, was no longer afraid of the evil man. "If he stays, then I go," she said. Señor Mora became very angry. He beat Laura.

After that day, Laura couldn't leave her bed. "Mama, I'm dying," she whispered. "Promise me you will change your ways and leave that man. God will help you." Laura's mother wept. She made up her mind to leave Señor Mora forever and to begin her life again with Jesus.

Laura died on January 22, 1904. She was just twelve years old. Pope John Paul II beatified her on September 3, 1988. Her feast day is January 22.

Blessed Laura, you weren't afraid to stand up for what is right. Give me the courage to avoid sinful situations and to help others avoid sin, too.

Saint Pauline of the Agonizing Heart of Jesus

1865–1942

"Trust in God...and never, never let yourself be discouraged...be faithful and forge ahead!"

Amabile Lucia Visintainer was born in Italy in 1865. When she was ten years old, her family, along with many others, moved to Brazil. These poor immigrants hoped to make a better life in South America. They settled in the village of Vigolo.

As she was growing up, Amabile learned how important it was to help others. She received her First Communion at the age of twelve. After that, she taught religious education classes to younger children. She also visited the sick with her mother and helped clean the church every week.

When Amabile was twenty-five, she and her friend, Virginia, went to live with and care for a woman who was dying of cancer. From this beginning, they established a new Congregation. They called it the Little Sisters of the Immaculate Conception. When she made her vows, Amabile took the new name Sister Pauline of the Agonizing Heart of Jesus.

Sister Pauline was soon named superior general. This was a great responsibility. Mother Pauline's Congregation grew quickly. Many other young women wanted to serve God and those in need.

The sisters lived in extreme poverty. They cared for orphans, the sick, and the dying. They helped the elderly and the children of former slaves. Even though Mother Pauline was head of her community, she always worked alongside her sisters. She bathed, fed, clothed, and prayed with those who could not provide for themselves.

Mother Pauline saw Jesus in everyone she served. Helping others filled her with deep happiness. "The presence of God is so intimate to me that it seems impossible for me to lose it; and such presence gives my soul a joy which I cannot describe," she said.

Some of her sisters didn't like the way Mother Pauline was doing things. They complained about her to the archbishop. In 1909, the archbishop asked Mother Pauline to step down as superior general. He told her she was to go to work at the Hospice of St. Vincent de Paul in a nearby town. She would no longer have an active role in her Congregation.

Mother Pauline was surprised at this decision. She was very sad to leave the Mother House in the Ipiranga district of São Paulo. Mother Pauline put the needs of her Congregation above her own. She was humble and obedient. Quietly she moved to the Hospice. There she continued to care for the sick and dying. She spent all her spare time praying for the needy and for the sisters of her Congregation.

Nine years later, the superior general of the Congregation asked Mother Pauline to come back to live at the Mother House. She lived there for the last years of her life, praying and always taking loving care of her sisters who were ill.

Before her death in 1942, she developed diabetes and became blind. Then her right arm had to be amputated. Through illness and sufferings, Mother Pauline always kept her strong faith. She was devoted to Jesus in the Eucharist, to the Blessed Mother, and to Saint Joseph. Today, the Little Sisters of the Immaculate Conception continue her work in Argentina, Chile, Nicaragua, Chad, Zambia, Mozambique, and Italy.

Pope John Paul II beatified Mother Pauline in Saõ Paulo, Brazil, in 1991. He canonized her on May 19, 2002. Saint Pauline is Brazil's first saint. Her feast day is July 9.

Saint Pauline, you show us how to remain humble and serve Jesus even in the face of problems. Help me to trust Jesus when things don't go my way.

The North American Martyrs

Saint John de Brébeuf, Saint Anthony Daniel,
Saint Isaac Jogues, Saint Charles Garnier,
Saint Noel Chabanel, Saint Gabriel Lalemant,
Saint René Goupil, and Saint John de Lalande

"The spread of faith in North America was consecrated
by the blood of the eight North American Martyrs."
— Pope Pius XI

When French explorers traveled to Canada and the northern part of the United States, missionaries came with them. These Jesuit and Franciscan priests hoped to settle in the New World. They were willing to suffer poverty and hardship in order to bring the Word of God to people of the First Nations and to Native Americans.

European settlers brought with them diseases that were new to North America. Large numbers of native people began to die from these diseases. Many tribes became angry and mistakenly blamed the missionaries for the deaths, for poor harvests, and for other bad luck. Other tribes were more willing to accept the teachings of the missionaries.

Father Isaac Jogues and his lay companions, René Goupil and John de Lalande, were French Jesuit missionaries. They traveled through regions known as New France in Canada and the northern United States. They loved the native people and worked very hard to bring Jesus to them.

The Hurons called the Jesuit priests "Blackrobes." Many of the Huron people decided to become Catholics. The missionaries set up chapels and schools. They learned the native languages and were treated as friends.

Another tribe, the Iroquois, were bitter enemies of the Hurons. The Iroquois people were angry with the French missionaries for bringing Christian customs to New France. They believed the missionaries were interfering with cultural traditions and beliefs. In 1642, the Iroquois attacked the Huron nation and kidnapped Father Jogues and René Goupil.

Their captors brought the missionaries to several different Iroquois villages. At each village they were beaten and tortured. René was killed with a tomahawk after making the Sign of the Cross on the forehead of a child.

Father Jogues remained a captive for thirteen months. During this time, he was often able to secretly teach and baptize other captives. Some of the Iroquois were his friends, and they quietly tried to make his life easier. One elderly woman gave him healing medicine and protected him whenever she could.

Finally, Father Jogues escaped. With the help of Dutch settlers, he made his way back to France. Soon this brave priest returned to the New World to continue his missionary work. Several years later, in 1646, he and John de Lalande were captured and killed.

Father John de Brébeuf, Father Anthony Daniel, and Father Gabriel Lalemant continued to establish Catholic communities among the Huron tribes. In 1648 and 1649, angry Iroquois tribes raided the peaceful settlements of the Hurons. The three Jesuit priests were among those killed, along with many Christian Hurons.

In 1649, Father Noel Chabanel was away from his Huron settlement when the Iroquois attacked and killed many men, women, and children. One of those killed was his companion, Father Charles Garnier. When Father Chabanel returned, he discovered the sad scene. He too was killed.

When the massacres were over, the surviving Hurons and missionaries found peace in what is now northern Michigan.

Pope Pius XI canonized the eight North American Martyrs in 1930. Their feast day outside of Canada is October 19. In Canada it is celebrated on September 26.

North American Martyrs, you never stopped preaching the Word of God. Help me to love and live this Word every day.

Blessed Marie of the Incarnation Guyard

1599–1672

"Nothing prevents the blessed soul's enjoyment of God's presence."

Marie Guyard was born in Tours, France, in 1599. She was the daughter of a baker and his wife. Marie loved to go to church. Every week, she memorized the homilies given by the priests at Mass. "I'm going to become a nun," she told her parents.

When she was seventeen, however, her parents persuaded her to marry Claude Martin, a silk manufacturer. A short time later, she had a son, Claude. After two years of marriage, Marie's husband died.

Marie and her baby moved back to her parents' house. Marie helped in her father's bakery and worked as an embroiderer. When her sister and her brother-in-law needed a bookkeeper for their shipping company, Marie and Claude moved in with them. Soon Marie was the company manager. But she was troubled.

"God is calling me to the convent," she told her sister, "but Claude needs a mother."

"I love him as my own child," her sister replied. "If God is calling you, I will care for your son." After years of prayer, Marie finally left Claude in the care of her sister and entered the Ursuline convent at Tours.

Twelve-year-old Claude was angry at first. He got together a group of his friends and tried to storm the convent and "free" his mother, but that didn't work. In time, after many conversations with his mother, and because of the loving care of his aunt, Claude was able to understand his mother's calling. He developed a deep love for Jesus and became a Benedictine priest. Later, he wrote his mother's life story.

Marie made her final vows as Sister Marie of the Incarnation. Not long after, the Blessed Mother appeared to her in a vision. Mary showed her a large country of mountains and forests. She asked Sister Marie to build a new convent there in the name of Jesus and Mary. Sister Marie was told by Mary that she would save many souls. In 1639, Sister Marie and two other sisters who desired to be missionaries were allowed to sail to New France, which is now Quebec, Canada.

The ocean journey was long and dangerous. When the sisters finally arrived, the settlers of New France rejoiced. For the first three years, the sisters, with Sister Marie as the superior, lived in a little house in the Lower Town. Then Mother Marie and her companions were able to build a convent.

In order to serve the people of the First Nations by teaching them about Jesus, Mother Marie learned their languages and taught them to her sisters. Mother Marie learned the languages so well that she wrote Algonquin, Iroquois, Montagnais, and Ouendat dictionaries. She even wrote a catechism in Iroquois!

Life was very difficult in the new country. Winters were bitterly cold, and many settlers died. The people of the First Nations suffered greatly from the diseases that Europeans brought to their land. Besides teaching, Mother Marie and the sisters spent much time caring for the sick, especially during the smallpox epidemic. In 1650, the Ursuline convent burned to the ground. Mother Marie didn't give up. A year later, the convent was rebuilt.

Mother Marie of the Incarnation Guyard died in Quebec in 1672, at the age of seventy-three. She is known as "the mother of the Canadian Church." Pope John Paul II beatified her in 1980. Her feast day is April 30.

Blessed Marie of the Incarnation, you made difficult decisions in order to do God's will. Help me to make the right choices, even when it's hard.

Blessed Kateri Tekakwitha

1656–1680

"I send you a treasure; guard her well."
— Letter from Father de Lamberville about Kateri Tekakwitha

In 1656, a baby girl was born to a Christian Algonquin woman and a Mohawk warrior. They named their baby Tekakwitha.

Tekakwitha had unusual parents. Her mother had been kidnapped by the Mohawks and taken by the warrior as his wife. Although her mother was not allowed to practice her Catholic faith, she set a wonderful example to Tekakwitha of living in peace and love.

When Tekakwitha was four years old, her parents and her baby brother died of smallpox, a disease brought to the New World by Europeans. Tekakwitha also caught smallpox, but she recovered. The disease left her face badly scarred and her vision blurred. For the rest of her life, Tekakwitha saw only shadows. Sunshine hurt her eyes.

Tekakwitha was raised by her aunt and uncle. She learned to pound corn to make flour. She embroidered designs on headbands, leggings, and belts. But her relatives could see that Tekakwitha was different. It wasn't just her poor sight or scars that set her apart from the others. Tekakwitha had a peaceful way about her. Shy and quiet by nature, she was cheerful and never let her own sufferings weigh on others.

After a peace treaty between the Mohawks and the French was signed, missionaries began to visit the Mohawk community. Tekakwitha was at first very careful around the missionaries. She knew that her uncle did not trust them. Soon, however, Tekakwitha went to the priests. She began to study the Catholic faith. She was baptized on Easter Sunday. Tekakwitha took the baptismal name Kateri, in honor of Saint Catherine of Siena. Kateri decided to model her life after Saint Catherine.

Kateri's Mohawk family did not understand the ways of the Church. Kateri's long hours of prayer, attachment to the Rosary, and devotion to the Eucharist upset her aunt and uncle. The other Mohawks made fun of her.

At that time, all young Mohawk women were expected to marry and have children. When Kateri announced that she would not marry, the members of her tribe became angry. The tribal elders would no longer allow her to eat. One day a young male warrior even ran at her with a tomahawk.

One of the missionary priests, Father de Lamberville, was worried about Kateri's safety. He secretly arranged for her to leave the Mohawk tribe and travel 200 miles to the Christian Algonquin tribe of her mother. Kateri left the Mohawk village at night and traveled alone on foot for three months. Finally, she reached her mother's former tribe in Canada. The Algonquins welcomed her.

Kateri's short life with her new family was a model of Christian virtue. She lived a life of prayer and penance, and she cared for the aged and sick. She attended Mass every day. Many Algonquins, as well as the missionaries, said Kateri was an example of a good Christian woman. Her kindness and simple manner helped to spread God's message throughout the New World. She became known as the "Lily of the Mohawks."

Kateri grew ill and died at the age of twenty-four. A wonderful transformation took place at the moment of her death. Her skin brightened and glowed, and the scars on her face disappeared. Her body became as beautiful as her soul.

Pope John Paul II beatified Kateri Tekakwitha on June 22, 1980. She is the first native North American to be declared blessed by the Roman Catholic Church.

Blessed Kateri, you are a model for all those who hold to their faith in spite of hardship. Help me to be as strong in my faith as you were.

Blessed François de Laval

1623–1708

"It is necessary to put our faith in the power of God."

François de Laval was born in 1863 to parents of high French nobility. He and his six brothers and sisters were educated in the best Catholic schools in France. François was a prayerful and hardworking student. "It is my desire to spread God's word," he once said in class. "Consider the priesthood," his teacher responded, "and then allow God to lead you." François had great faith in God. He entered the seminary, and in 1647, at the age of twenty-four, he was ordained a priest.

Father de Laval served in local parishes. In 1658, after eleven years as a priest, he was ordained a bishop. When Jesuit missionaries began organizing religious communities in New France, now Quebec, Canada, they asked for guidance. King Louis XIV himself asked the Holy Father to send Bishop François de Laval to serve as the first bishop of Quebec. The request was granted. Bishop de Laval would travel to New France to take charge of all the mission territories claimed by the French in the New World.

Bishop de Laval's journey from France to Quebec took several months by ship. It was a long voyage over dangerous seas. The day the bishop's ship arrived, all the settlers of the colony were waiting for him on the wharf. Bells rang, cannons boomed, and the people cheered! Bishop de Laval was greatly moved.

One big problem in New France, the bishop soon realized, was the trading of alcohol to people of the First Nations. The settlers provided the tribes with liquor in return for valuable furs. The alcohol had a terrible effect on the health of the native people. Bishop de Laval asked the government to pass a law forbidding the trading, but he was not successful. Finally, he made a hard decision. He announced that Catholics who continued in this trading would be excommunicated from the Church.

This decision angered many in the community. Bishop François suffered from their anger, but he knew that it was his duty to protect the people of the First Nations. He cared deeply about their health and welfare. He wanted everyone to understand that none of God's people should be treated unfairly. Finally, twenty years later, the king of France outlawed the trading of alcohol.

Bishop de Laval was a wonderful bishop. He worked hard to organize all the missions in New France. Even though he was very intelligent, he was very humble. In times of difficulty he always prayed for God's help and guidance. He built churches and schools throughout his immense diocese. He was a friend to all, including government officials, French settlers, and the people of the First Nations.

Toward the end of his long life, Bishop de Laval became frail and ill. He still made long trips on foot, paddling his canoe along the river, and traveling on snowshoes to visit the sick and dying. He kept his room bare and slept on boards. In 1708, when he died at the age of eighty-five, Bishop de Laval was penniless. He had given away all he had to the poor.

Pope John Paul II beatified Bishop François de Laval, who is known as "the father of the country," in June of 1980. His feast day is May 6.

Blessed François, you were humble and put the needs of others before your own. Help me to be caring and loving to all who need my help.

Saint Marie-Marguérite d'Youville

1701–1771

"Lord, make known to me the way I should walk."

Marie-Marguérite de Lajemmerais was born on October 15, 1701, in Varennes, Quebec, Canada. When she was seven years old, her father died. The family was left very poor. Marguérite attended a convent school run by the Ursuline Sisters. When she finished school, she helped to educate her younger brothers and sisters at home on the family farm. She also worked to support her family by making and selling lace.

When she was twenty years old, Marguérite married a wealthy man named François d'Youville. The marriage was not a happy one. François proved to be a dishonest man. He made his money from the sale of alcohol to people of the First Nations. He didn't take care of his family. Still, Marguérite tried to be a good wife. She had six children, but four of them died as infants. After eight years, her husband became very ill. Marguérite nursed him devotedly, but he too died. Marguérite and her children were left with no money.

Marguérite worked hard to pay off her husband's debts. She also made sure her children received a good religious education. When they were older, both her sons decided to become priests. After her first son left for the seminary, Marguérite talked to her spiritual director, Father Gabriel du Lescoat. "I feel called to provide works of mercy, to serve others," she told him. Father Gabriel encouraged her, telling her, "God has destined you for great work."

Marguérite opened her home to all in need. She took in the homeless. She welcomed a blind woman who had nowhere else to live. She cared for the sick and fed the hungry. Soon three other young women joined her. They shared her love and concern for all God's people.

Five years later, Marguérite and her companions established a new religious Congregation, the Sisters of Charity. They were also known as the Grey Nuns, because of the habits they wore.

After much prayer and creative fundraising, the Sisters of Charity took over the Charon Brothers Hospital of Montreal. The building was very shabby. The hospital was heavily in debt and on the verge of closing.

Mother Marguérite worked to pay off the many bills. The sisters prayed, baked, sewed, and bargained. They restored the hospital and opened it to everyone who was sick. Later, the Sisters of Charity opened the first orphanage in North America.

Mother Marguérite and her sisters believed the way to reach heaven was through prayer and service to others. They raised enough money to purchase several farms. Homeless families came to live and work on the farms. The Sisters of Charity taught religion classes for the children.

After the French and Indian War, there was much religious persecution in Quebec. The Sisters of Charity suffered greatly. Still, Marguérite and her sisters prayed and worked hard, even when their beloved hospital burned to the ground in 1765. Nothing could destroy their faith and courage. A new hospital was soon built. Mother Marguérite continued to fight for the rights of the poor. Whether people could afford it or not, everyone received care. Mother Marguérite became known as "the mother of the poor."

Mother Marguérite died at the age of seventy. The Sisters of Charity continued to grow throughout Canada and the United States. Soon communities of Grey Nuns were begun in Alaska, China, Japan, Africa, New Guinea, South America, the Bahamas, the Dominican Republic, and Haiti.

Pope John Paul II canonized Marie-Marguérite d'Youville on December 9, 1990. She is the first native-born Canadian to be elevated to sainthood. Her feast day is October 16.

Saint Marie-Marguérite, you believed that prayer and loving service go together. Help me to show my love for God by the way I love and serve others.

Blessed Marie-Rose Durocher

1811–1849

"May the love and grace of God unite us forever."

Melanie Eulalie Durocher was born in 1811 in the little village of St. Antoine-sur-Richlieu, Quebec, Canada. Her parents were farmers, and she was their tenth child. They called her Eulalie. She was a fun-loving child with lots of energy. Her family loved her very much.

When she was old enough, Eulalie went to a religious boarding school. After a short time, she had to return home due to illness. Eulalie cared for the family horse, Caesar. She rode the horse to Mass every day. She also rode him to visit the sick. Riding in the fresh air improved Eulalie's health. Soon she was strong and well again.

When Eulalie was eighteen, her mother died. Her brother, Theophile, was the pastor of a church in the neighboring village of Beloeil. He asked his sister and their father to come to live with him. Eulalie took charge of housekeeping duties at the rectory. She helped in the parish and taught religious classes. She organized retreats for young women and held special activities for children. She became known for her love of prayer and for her kindness.

Eulalie had a special interest in the religious education of young women, and she started the first Canadian parish sodality. She knew young women were very important. They would be the future mothers in Catholic homes.

When Eulalie was thirty, the bishop of Montreal asked her to begin a new religious community. It was to be called the Sisters of the Holy Names of Jesus and Mary. This Congregation would be dedicated to educating the poor, especially young women, in rural areas of Quebec.

Eulalie's brother, Father Theophile, wasn't sure she could handle the responsibility. "This is something you'd better think about carefully," he said sternly. Eulalie prayed and meditated. "I am meant to do this," she told her brother.

Soon she and three other young women moved into their new convent. A year later, Eulalie made her religious vows. She took the name Sister Marie-Rose. The bishop named her mother superior of the new convent. The motto of the Congregation was "Jesus and Mary, my strength and my glory."

For six years, Mother Marie-Rose led her community in teaching the Catholic faith to children. They founded schools in the surrounding villages. The sisters maintained the highest standards of education. In addition to religion, they taught music, art, and homemaking. They worked very hard.

Mother Marie-Rose and her sisters were motivated by love of God, devotion to Jesus and Mary, and concern for the educational needs of society. In spite of lack of money and many other problems, the new Congregation continued to grow.

In 1849, at the age of thirty-eight, Mother Marie-Rose became ill and died of pneumonia. Today, the work of the Sisters of the Holy Names of Jesus and Mary has expanded. They continue their mission of educating children. They teach adults and minister to the poor and disadvantaged in Canada, the United States, South Africa, Brazil, Peru, and Haiti.

Pope John Paul II beatified Mother Marie-Rose Durocher on May 23, 1982. On the same day, he also declared another Canadian, Brother André Bessette, to be blessed. Fifty thousand people, including over two thousand Canadians, attended the ceremony in Saint Peter's Square at the Vatican.

Blessed Marie-Rose Durocher's feast day is celebrated on October 6.

Blessed Marie-Rose, you sacrificed and worked very hard to bring education to children. Help me to try my best at school, even on days when it isn't easy.

Blessed Marie-Leonie Paradis

1840–1912

*"My daughters, do not weary in day-to-day tasks.
Our principal work is charity."*

Alodie-Virginie Paradis was born in 1840 in the village of L'Acadie, Quebec, Canada. Her family called her Élodie. Élodie's parents were poor, but they were very devout Catholics. They wanted their daughter to have a good religious education.

When Élodie was nine, they sent her to the boarding school of the Sisters of Notre Dame. Élodie loved her school, as well as the sisters who were her teachers. At the age of fifteen, she decided to enter the Congregation of the Holy Cross. Her father was not happy.

"My daughter, the religious life is not for you," he insisted. "Please come home." Élodie was firm. She told her father, "This is not only my decision, but God's will." In time, Élodie's family came to accept her religious vocation. When she was seventeen, she made her vows, taking the religious name Marie-Leonie.

Sister Marie-Leonie taught school in Canada. Soon, her superiors sent her to the Saint Vincent de Paul orphanage in New York. Sister Marie-Leonie loved teaching and taking care of the children. "Children respond best to love and gentleness," she told her sisters. "Remember, we are their family now." The orphans loved the smiling sister who was always ready with a hug.

After eight years, Sister Marie-Leonie was transferred to Indiana. There she continued to teach. She became known for her hard work and kindness, for her dedication to prayer, and for her devotion to the Holy Eucharist.

Twenty years after she entered religious life, Sister Marie-Leonie was called from the United States back to New Brunswick, Canada. She was assigned to teach at Saint Joseph College, a school for women. While there, Sister Marie-Leonie was led by God to found a new religious Congregation.

In 1880, the small sister with the big smile became mother superior of the Society of the Little Sisters of the Holy Family. The special work of the sisters was taking care of the household needs of priests. Besides cooking, cleaning, and sewing, the Little Sisters of the Holy Family supported the priests with their prayers. Through their service of the Church and its priests, the new Congregation prospered.

Priests and sisters alike soon knew Mother Marie-Leonie as a woman with a loving heart. She was always ready to listen and to help anyone with problems. She took care of the people who are most often overlooked— those who care for others. Priests and sisters flocked to her for encouragement and advice so they could continue ministering to those who needed them. One priest said, "Mother Marie-Leonie always has open arms and a listening heart. She has good and honest laughter on her lips, seeing God in everyone and treating them with great respect and love."

Mother Marie-Leonie continued her work with priests and sisters until she died in 1912, at the age of seventy-two. The Little Sisters of the Holy Family now have sixty-seven convents in Canada, the United States, Rome, and Honduras.

In 1984, Pope John Paul II traveled to Montreal, Canada, to beatify Mother Marie-Leonie. He called her "a humble person among humble ones." The little sister with the big smile spent her life making sure that all people, young and old, were cared for as members of God's family. Her feast day is May 4.

Blessed Marie-Leonie, you gave support to all who needed it by listening and smiling. Help me to cheerfully give the gift of my time and love to those in need.

Blessed Frederic Janssoone

1838–1916

*"I shall never forget the gaze of our Blessed Mother...
it is engraved upon my soul."*

Frederic Janssoone was born in Ghyvelde, French Flanders, in 1838. His parents were Flemish farmers, and he was the youngest of thirteen children. When Frederic was nine years old, his father died. After his mother died in 1861, Frederic entered the seminary, and he was ordained a Franciscan priest in 1870.

Father Frederic served for a short time as a military chaplain, caring for soldiers injured in the Franco-Prussian War. After that, he began a religious magazine. He also founded a convent, organized retreats, and started many Third Order (Secular) Franciscan groups for lay people. Then, in 1876, he was sent to the Holy Land.

While serving in the Holy Land, Father Frederic gave retreats and led pilgrimages. In Jerusalem, he revived an old custom among pilgrims of following the Way of the Cross along the path our Lord took to Calvary. He helped in the restoration of churches. He preached at the Holy Sepulcher where Jesus was buried and resurrected. During this period of time, he developed a deep devotion to the Blessed Mother.

In 1881, Father Frederic traveled to Canada. Many people came to hear him preach about his years in the Holy Land. He brought with him a number of relics. Often he would touch sick people with one of the relics and then pray with them. Many of them became well.

Father Frederic became known as a miracle worker. Whenever he heard this, his reply was, "I do not cure. Miracles are due to God's love and the faith of the people."

In 1888, Father Frederic preached at the dedication of the Shrine of Our Lady of the Rosary at Cap-de-Madeleine, Quebec. That night, Father Frederic and two others prayed at the altar before a statue of the Blessed Mother. The statue had been sculpted with the eyes looking downward. As the three prayed, the eyes of the Virgin were raised, and, for several minutes, gazed straight at them!

For the rest of his life, Father Frederic treasured this memory. The beautiful eyes of the Blessed Mother inspired him in many writings, sermons, and retreats.

One cold winter day, Father Frederic wanted to visit someone who was sick. He asked a young man to pick him up and take him in his sleigh across the ice of a frozen river. When night fell, the young man was dismayed to find that the ice had melted, leaving him with no way to drive the priest back. Father Frederic told him not to worry and to go on home.

The next day, Father Frederic was somehow back at the rectory. No one ever found out how he got there!

Father Frederic would say only, "Oh, the Mother of God provided for my transport!"

During his twenty-eight years in Canada, Father Frederic encouraged the construction of several life-sized Stations of the Cross. He also began many Secular Franciscan groups, serving as their spiritual assistant. He wrote and published a number of articles and biographies of saints.

Throughout his life, Father Frederic prayed intently. He was greatly loved by all, and always remained humble, joyful, and peaceful. After many years of illness, Father Frederic Janssoone died in Montreal in 1916. He was seventy-eight years old. Pope John Paul II beatified him on September 25, 1988. His feast day is August 5.

Blessed Frederic, God blessed you with many talents and gifts that you shared with others. Help me to recognize my talents and use them to do good, too.

Blessed André Bessette

1845–1937

"Place yourself in God's hands. He will not abandon you."

In 1845, Alfred Bessette was born to French Canadian parents near Montreal. His was a busy, happy home filled with work, prayer, and devotion to God. But when Alfred's father died suddenly in an accident, everything changed.

Shortly after his father's death, Alfred's mother fell ill with tuberculosis. She died when Alfred was twelve. He and his eleven brothers and sisters had to go to live with different relatives. Alfred went to live with his uncle, who was a farmer. The uncle believed in hard work, but not in basic schooling. As a teenager, Alfred was barely able to read or write.

Alfred spent his early adulthood drifting from job to job. He spent time as a farmhand, shoemaker, baker, blacksmith, and factory worker. Alfred's health was poor, and none of these jobs lasted long. Sometimes he felt like a failure. But in his heart, he knew God had great plans ahead.

Alfred had a special devotion to the Holy Eucharist and to Saint Joseph, the foster father of Jesus. He often prayed to Saint Joseph to help direct his life. He had visions of a beautiful church that would someday be built in honor of Saint Joseph on Mount Royal in Montreal.

When he was twenty-five, Alfred entered the Congregation of the Holy Cross. When he made his vows, he chose the name André. Brother André was given the humble job of doorkeeper and messenger at Notre Dame College in Montreal. He also worked in the laundry. He was considered a simple brother, unable to do difficult tasks. But God knew differently.

In the 1890s the Congregation of the Holy Cross tried to buy land on Mount Royal, but, for several years, was unsuccessful. Brother André and his friends climbed the steep slope to plant medals of Saint Joseph on the hillside. Soon after, the owners agreed to sell the land to the Congregation!

Brother André built a small shrine in honor of Saint Joseph on the hillside. Here he praised God and begged Saint Joseph to help him be of service to others. Whenever he heard someone was ill, Brother André prayed for a recovery. He visited each sick person and blessed him or her with oil taken from a lamp in the shrine. Often, the sick person would get better. News of the brother with healing powers began to spread. Soon hundreds of people came to his door hoping for cures.

Not everyone in his community was happy with Brother André's special gifts. Some wondered if he was only pretending to heal people. But Brother André remained peaceful. He continued to pray with the sick and anoint them with oil from Saint Joseph's shrine. When he was insulted or made fun of, he always replied, "I do not cure. Jesus heals through Saint Joseph." Before he died, Brother André was receiving over 80,000 letters a year from people seeking his prayers and healing.

In 1924, Brother André began the construction of a magnificent basilica dedicated to Saint Joseph on Mount Royal. Saint Joseph's Oratory took fifty years to complete. Brother André Bessette, a simple man of God, died in 1937 at the age of ninety-two. He is buried in the church he built. More than a million people are said to have climbed Mount Royal to pay their respects at his funeral. Pope John Paul II beatified Brother André Bessette on May 23, 1982. His feast day is January 6.

Blessed André, you showed how even a simple person can do great things in Jesus' name. Help me to be God's hands on earth.

Saint Teresa of Jesus of Los Andes

1900–1920

"Dealing with the world always leaves an emptiness that Our Lord fills completely when I'm with him in church."

On a July day in 1900, a little girl was born in Santiago, Chile. Her wealthy parents named her Juana Enriqueta Josefina of the Sacred Hearts Fernandez Solar. This was a big name for a tiny baby! Her family and friends called her Juanita.

Along with her sisters and brothers, Juanita attended the finest Catholic schools. She was spoiled and always wanted the best of everything. Then something happened to change her. When she made her First Communion, the Lord spoke to her. At that time Juanita didn't think this was unusual. She thought that Jesus spoke to everyone at First Communion! From then on, Juanita lived differently. She began to study the Bible, pray intensely, and attend daily Mass.

Juanita felt drawn to give her life to God. Holiness became her goal. As a teenager, she read the autobiography of Saint Thérèse of Lisieux, the Carmelite nun. This deepened Juanita's desire to serve God. She wanted to be like Saint Thérèse. She was also inspired by the life of Blessed Elizabeth of the Trinity, another holy Carmelite nun.

When she prayed, Juanita became very still and listened as God spoke in her heart. Her pastor encouraged her to write down what God told her. She kept her diaries for the rest of her life.

Juanita had both an unusual intelligence and a great capacity for love. She was sympathetic to those in need, cheerful, and happy. Even adults came to Juanita when they needed help.

When she was seventeen, Juanita visited the tiny Carmelite Monastery of the Holy Spirit in the township of Los Andes, about fifty miles from her home. She wrote in her diary, "The first visit to my small convent filled my soul with peace." It was to this monastery, she knew, that God was calling her. Mother Angelica Teresa, the prioress, recognized in Juanita "a greatness of soul." She even declared that Juanita was "born to be a Carmelite." At the age of nineteen, Juanita entered the Carmelite Order, taking the name Sister Teresa of Jesus.

In the monastery, Sister Teresa continued her life of deep prayer and meditation. She also continued to keep her spiritual diary. Sister Teresa was an inspiration to all the sisters. She found joy in giving herself totally to God through prayer and sacrifice. "I am God's," she wrote in her diary. "He created me and is my beginning and my end."

Shortly after entering the convent, and just three months before her twentieth birthday, Sister Teresa contracted typhus. She became very ill. On April 7, 1920, she was allowed to make her religious vows, because she was in danger of death. Under usual circumstances, she would have had to wait six months longer. Sister Teresa died, with great joy, as a Carmelite nun.

Every year, thousands of people travel to her shrine in Los Andes to pray. Pope John Paul II canonized Sister Teresa of Jesus in 1993. She is the first Chilean to be declared a saint. Her feast day is April 12.

Saint Teresa, you knew how to laugh, to play, to serve, and to love with all of your heart. Help me, too, to live the life God has given me as fully as possible.

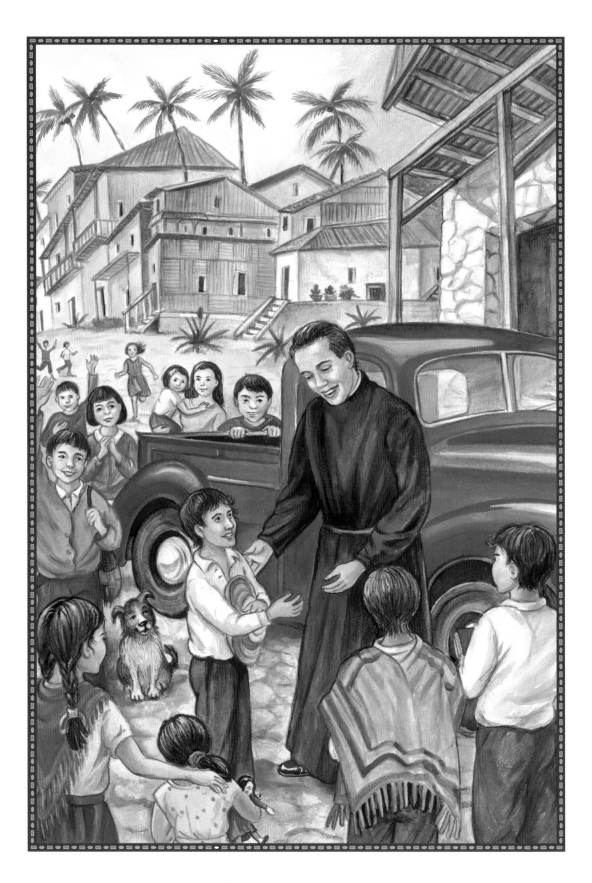

Saint Alberto Hurtado Cruchaga

1901–1952

"I am happy, Lord, happy!"

Alberto Hurtado Cruchaga was born in 1901 in Vina del Mar, Chile. When he was four years old, his father died. Alberto and his brother were raised in the care of their loving mother. The little family was very poor. Alberto's mother had to sell the family farm in order for them to survive.

Alberto was a hard worker and did well in school. In 1923, he earned a scholarship to the Jesuit College in Santiago. While he studied at the college, Alberto began working to help the needy and homeless people of Santiago. Every Sunday afternoon he visited them in the poorest sections of the city. Alberto knew from his own experience how hard it is to live in poverty.

After his ordination in 1933, Father Alberto continued to work for the poor of Chile. He gave retreats and sermons, encouraging people to help the poor and homeless. He told of homeless men, women, and children living under bridges, right in their own country.

With the donations he received, Father Alberto built El Hogar de Cristo, which means "Christ's House." The priest was often seen in his little green pick-up truck, offering homeless persons rides to El Hogar. There they would receive food and a night's sleep in a real bed.

El Hogar offered shelter and hope to the many abandoned children of Santiago. Father Alberto also began trade schools. By learning a trade, the poor were enabled to find good jobs and care for themselves and their families.

Father Alberto had a special way of communicating that was simple and direct. He counseled young men studying for the priesthood. He talked to the wealthy, the poor, and children of all ages. Father Alberto saw greed for money or possessions as an obstacle to loving God. He believed that all people should help one another, not just themselves. He explained that this is the way to love and to serve God.

Father Alberto wrote many books. One of the most famous, *Is Chile a Catholic Country?*, was published in 1941. That same year, he became the national chaplain to the Catholic Action youth movement.

Father Alberto also encouraged families to pray together. He was especially encouraging to young men who were considering entering the priesthood. He knew that the Church would need more and more priests in South America.

Father Alberto often worked with the government, finding and creating jobs for the poor. He began the Chilean Trade Union Association to ensure the good

Christian treatment of workers. He also started a monthly magazine called *Mensaje,* or *Message.* This magazine was dedicated to explaining the Church's teachings on social issues. Father Alberto strongly believed in social justice. Social justice asks for fair treatment of all people, whether they are born rich or poor.

Just fifteen years after his ordination, Father Alberto developed cancer. He lived for only a few months, in terrible pain. Although he suffered a great deal, he still found joy in God and his faith. "I am happy, Lord," his nurses heard him say many times. This beloved priest died on August 18, 1952.

Father Alberto Hurtado Cruchaga was canonized on October 23, 2005. His feast day is August 18.

Saint Alberto, you knew that all people are equal in the eyes of God. You worked to make sure that everyone was treated with dignity and respect. Help me to always be kind and fair to others.

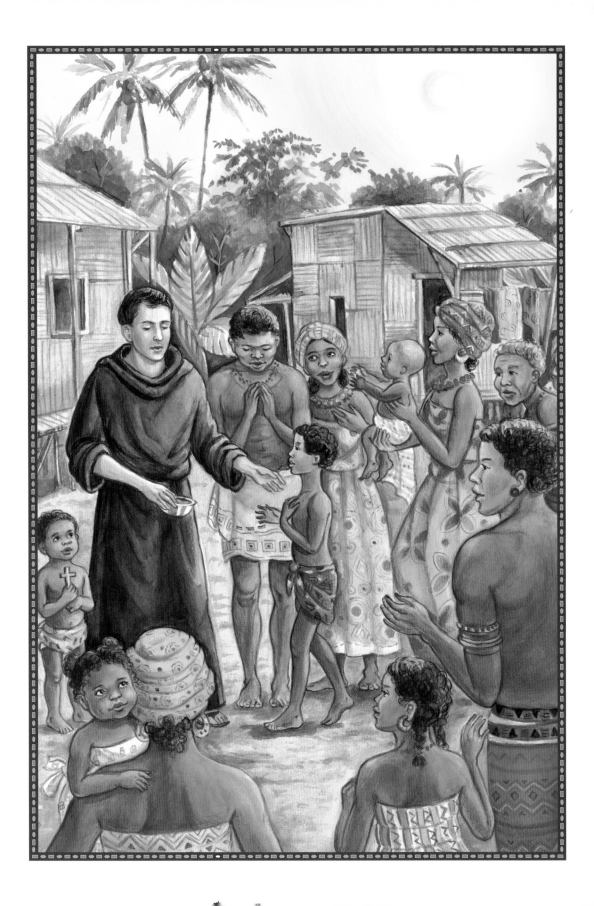

Saint Peter Claver

1580–1654

"We must love nothing but God, or if we love anything else, we must love it only for his sake."

Peter Claver was born in 1580 in Catalonia, Spain. Peter studied at the Jesuit College in Barcelona. He joined the Society of Jesus in 1602 and was sent to Majorca. There he met a holy Jesuit brother named Alphonsus Rodriguez. Brother Alphonsus told Peter that he would someday care for African slaves in the New World. Peter spent many hours thinking and praying about this idea. Finally, he volunteered to go to the missions.

In 1610, Peter's superiors sent him to Colombia. After studying at Bogotá, Peter was transferred to Cartagena. He was ordained there in 1615. When he saw the conditions of the African slaves there, he knew what he had to do.

Cartagena was a seaport and a major center for the slave trade. In Father Claver's time, about 10,000 slaves passed through the port each year. Slaving ships picked up their captives on the coast of Africa. Then they brought them to Cartagena to be sold. The sea voyage lasted over two months. Conditions on board the ships were horrible. The African people were crowded in the darkness below deck. They did not have clean water to drink or enough food to eat. They had no warm clothing. They were beaten and neglected. On every voyage, many people got sick and died at sea.

When the ships landed, the frightened Africans didn't know where they were, or whether they would live or die. Father Claver met the ships and went on board, bringing food and medicine. He washed and tended their wounds. He comforted and blessed the dying. Sometimes he carried the sick ashore in his arms. Father Claver's tender care was the first kindness the Africans had known since they were kidnapped from their homes.

The priest made himself the "slave of the slaves forever." He ministered to the slaves for forty years. Besides the physical care he gave them, Father Claver taught them about Jesus and baptized those who wished to become Christians. It is recorded that he baptized at least 300,000 African slaves!

Father Claver also encouraged owners of slaves to treat them kindly, reminding them, "God has a good memory and will reward those who care for others." Some owners listened to him. Others became angry.

Many people were upset that Father Claver ministered to the African slaves. Some people would not enter churches where Africans received the sacraments. Father Claver knew that all people are equal in God's eyes. He preached in the public square and visited prisons and hospitals. Many times, he wrapped his own cloak around slaves who were sick or dying. He fought for laws to allow Christian marriages of slaves, and to keep families together.

Father Claver's work did not stop in Cartagena. Many slaves were sold to owners who lived far away in the countryside. Every year after Easter, Father Claver traveled for miles, over mountains, forests, and bogs, to visit the people he had baptized. In village after village, as slaves returned from their long days working in the fields, he was greeted with love.

When Father Claver died in 1654, people of all races attended his funeral. Pope Leo XIII canonized Father Peter Claver on January 15, 1888. On the same day, Father Claver's old friend, Brother Alphonsus Rodriguez, was also canonized. Saint Peter Claver's feast day is September 9.

Saint Peter, in your great love for God and your neighbor, you placed your life at the service of the slaves. I want to pray for and help people who are not treated fairly today.

Saint Anthony Mary Claret

1807–1870

*"The love of Christ arouses us, urges us to run,
and to fly, lifted on the wings of holy zeal."*

On Christmas Eve, in 1807, a son was born to Juan and Josepha Claret, in northern Spain. They named him Antonio, or Anthony. These deeply religious parents rejoiced at his birth. "He is destined to be a leader for Christ," they said.

Anthony was a happy child. In his youth, he worked at his father's trade of weaving. Later, he learned to operate a printing press. Later still, he realized his true vocation was to the priesthood. In 1935, Anthony was ordained.

Father Anthony served as a parish priest in his hometown of Sallent, Spain. Here he ministered to the poor, bringing to them his own faith, love, and hope in God. Four years later, he traveled to Rome, where he briefly entered the Jesuit Order as a novice. It was in Rome that he began the writings that would later make him famous. Because of poor health, he returned to Spain and became a pastor.

Father Anthony was a dedicated preacher and gave many retreats and conferences. His sermons and religious writings were very powerful. He had the loving heart of a missionary and was a true servant to his people. He became famous as a healer of both souls and bodies.

In 1848, Father Anthony was sent to the Canary Islands, off the coast of Africa. Because the crowds for his missions were too large for the churches, he often had to preach in public squares. People said a "remarkable light" surrounded him as he celebrated Mass. Father Anthony was beloved by his people. His dream was "to set the world on fire with God's love."

While in the Canary Islands, Father Anthony founded the Missionary Sons of the Immaculate Heart of Mary, later called the Claretians. This new religious Congregation was devoted to teaching. Father Anthony used his knowledge of printing to write, print, and publish over 200 books and pamphlets. He also helped to start the Religious Library, which produced thousands of publications.

At the age of forty-three, Father Anthony was named archbishop of Santiago, Cuba. He did not think he was worthy of such an important post, but said he would do his best. Because of his great devotion to the Blessed Mother, he took the name of Mary. He knew that Mary would always help him to be close to Jesus.

Archbishop Claret spent seven years ministering in Cuba. He traveled throughout the island, visiting parishes, administering the sacraments, and helping the people. He spoke out against slavery, which he saw as a great evil. This made some people angry. Threats were even made against his life, and one man tried to kill him. Archbishop Claret was seriously wounded, but he forgave the man for what he had done.

Archbishop Anthony Mary Claret became known as the "spiritual father of Cuba." In 1857, he returned to Spain. He continued his teaching and founded a science laboratory, a museum, schools of music and language, and an association of writers and artists. He also helped prepare for the First Vatican Council in Rome in 1869.

Anthony Mary Claret died in France at the age of sixty-two. Pope Pius XII declared him a saint on May 5, 1950. His feast day is October 23.

Saint Anthony, you were devoted to Mary, the Blessed Mother of God. Help me to grow in faith and remember that Mary will always bring me closer to Jesus.

Saint Pedro de San José Betancur

1626–1667

*"To serve the sick, the dying, the poor and homeless...
this is my glory."*

Pedro Betancur was born in 1626 on the island of Tenerife, Canary Islands, to a shepherd and his wife. Although the family was poor and Pedro received little education, his parents were religious and taught him the faith. Pedro helped his father herd sheep. Together they worked and prayed. Often, Pedro would use his time outdoors to meditate and pray. He learned to see God's presence in everything around him.

At the age of twenty-three, Pedro felt called to bring the message of Christ to the New World. In 1650, he left his country. When his ship reached Cuba, he ran out of money. He worked in Havana to earn more. A year later, he worked his way to Honduras on another ship. From there, he walked to Guatemala. When he reached Guatemala City, he knelt down, kissed the ground, and said, "I must live and die here."

In Guatemala City, Pedro was so poor he stood in line at the Franciscan friary to get bread every day. Friar

Fernando Espino, a famous missionary, became his friend. He got Pedro a job in a textile factory. In 1653, Pedro entered the Jesuit College, hoping to become a priest.

Pedro had received little formal education as a child. Studying was very difficult for him. Eventually he had to leave the college. Friar Fernando invited Pedro to join the Franciscans as a lay brother, but he decided to take private vows instead. Pedro joined the Third Order (Secular) of Saint Francis in 1655, taking the name Brother Pedro de San José.

From that time on, Brother Pedro dedicated himself to helping the poor. He did everything he could to help African slaves and the native people. He walked the streets of the rich section of the city, begging the wealthy to give money for the poor, the homeless, and the sick.

Soon Brother Pedro bought a small house. He used the house to teach the homeless to read and write. "This house will be called the Little House of Our Lady of Bethlehem," he said. "It will serve the poor sons and daughters of God. It will house them, teach them, and love them just as Our Blessed Mother cared for her infant son, Jesus, in Bethlehem."

Eventually, Brother Pedro established a hospital in Guatemala for the poor and homeless. He built chapels and shrines in the poor sections of the city. Men and women joined him to form the Bethlehemite Congregation, the first native religious community in America.

Many wondrous tales are told of Brother Pedro. Once, a poor man came up to him in the street. He told Brother

Pedro that his wife was very sick and his children were starving. Brother Pedro picked up a little green lizard from the ground and gave it to the man. It turned into a beautiful jewel. The man sold it and used the money to help his family. Years later, he grew so wealthy that he was able to buy back the jewel and return it to Brother Pedro. When he placed it in Brother Pedro's hand, it turned back into a lizard—and scurried away!

Brother Pedro de San José Betancur died at the age of forty-one. Pope John Paul II canonized him on July 30, 2002. He is the first Guatemalan saint. His feast day is April 25.

Saint Pedro, even though you were never able to become a priest, you helped so many people in so many ways. Help me to turn my disappointments into opportunities for doing good.

Saint Juan Diego

1474–1548

"I shall go and do your will...though I may not be believed."

The saint we know as Juan Diego was born to Aztec parents in Mexico in 1474, eighteen years before Columbus sailed to America. He was given the name Cuauhtlatoatzin, which means "the talking eagle." Cuauhtlatoatzin married and worked as a farmer, field worker, and mat maker. His wife died without leaving him any children. Although raised with no formal religious training, Cuauhtlatoatzin believed in a supreme power.

When Spanish Franciscan missionaries arrived in Mexico, Cuauhtlatoatzin learned about Jesus and the Catholic Church. At the age of fifty, he was baptized. Cuauhtlatoatzin's baptismal name was Juan Diego.

Juan Diego was often seen deep in prayer at daily Mass. He developed a strong devotion to the Blessed Mother and admired her loving obedience to God.

On December 9, 1531, on his walk to Mass, Juan heard beautiful music. As he reached the top of Tepeyac Hill, a lovely woman called to him, "Juan, where are you going?"

When he replied that he was going to Mass, the Lady smiled. "I am Mary, the Mother of God, who is the author of life, the creator of all things." She then asked Juan to have a chapel built there on the hill and promised, "I will give my love, compassion, help, and protection to all those who invoke my name."

Juan Diego hurried to the bishop to tell him about the apparition. Bishop Zumarraga did not believe the story! Disappointed, Juan returned to the Blessed Virgin, who was waiting for him.

"Go back to the bishop tomorrow," Mary instructed. "Tell him to build me the church that I ask for."

Juan obeyed. This time, Bishop Zumarraga asked for a sign that Mary had really appeared. Juan walked back to Tepeyac Hill, where he again met the Blessed Virgin. "The bishop wants a sign," Juan explained.

"Return here tomorrow, and I will give you a sign," Mary promised.

The next day, when Mary appeared, she told Juan to gather the roses he would find at the top of the hill. It was December 12. Juan knew there could be no roses at that time of year, but he obeyed. He walked to the rocky area she indicated, and sure enough, roses were growing! Juan picked them and wrapped them carefully in his *tilma,* a cloak made from cactus fibers.

Juan hurried back to the bishop. "The Blessed Mother left a miracle garden on the hill!" he exclaimed. He opened his *tilma* and the roses dropped to the floor. Bishop Zumarraga fell on his knees. Inside Juan Diego's *tilma* was a beautiful full-length picture of Mary!

"A chapel will be built on the hill," the bishop promised Juan. The miraculous *tilma* was placed in the chapel for all to see. In 1976, a new basilica was completed in the same location. Even though *tilma* cloth usually falls apart in twenty or thirty years, Juan Diego's *tilma* can still be seen today. It shows a pregnant woman with Aztec features and dress. An angel supports her. The moon is beneath her feet, and her blue mantle is covered with gold stars.

Our Lady of Guadalupe has come to symbolize the equality of all races. She is also the patroness of unborn children and of the Americas.

Juan Diego died at the age of seventy-four. He was canonized by Pope John Paul II in July 2002. His feast day is December 9.

Saint Juan, you passed on Mary's message even though at first it was not believed. Help me to be courageous and faithful in doing whatever God wants.

Blessed Miguel Agustín Pro

1891–1927

"Long live Christ the King!"

In 1891, Miguel Agustín Pro was born in Guadalupe, Mexico. He was one of ten children of devout Catholic parents. Miguel, called "Miguelito" by his family, was a happy boy. He was known for his practical jokes and good humor. He was also deeply spiritual.

When his older sister entered the convent, Miguel realized that he, too, had a religious vocation. When he was twenty years old, he began studying for the priesthood at a local Jesuit seminary. Three years later, because of the Mexican Revolution, he was forced to leave his country. The Mexican government had begun a terrible persecution of Catholics. Sisters, priests, and lay people who sheltered priests and sisters were punished. Many were injured and even killed.

Miguel attended seminaries in California, Nicaragua, and Spain. Finally, he was ordained in Belgium in 1925. Father Pro's health was not good, and he suffered from stomach problems. After a year in Belgium, his superiors allowed him to return to Mexico City to be near his family.

The Mexican government's persecution of Catholics was worse than ever. All the churches were closed. Priests and sisters had gone into hiding. Father Pro immediately began setting up Communion stations in private homes throughout the city. In this way, he secretly distributed Holy Communion to 300 Catholics a day.

Father Pro often disguised himself as he went from house to house. Dressed as a mechanic, a student, or even a businessman, he would walk a neighbor's dog and pretend to visit friends. He went out in the middle of the night disguised as a beggar or a street-sweeper. In reality, Father Pro was hearing confessions, baptizing infants, blessing marriages, and administering the Anointing of the Sick. Disguised as a policeman, he even brought Holy Communion to prisoners in the police station!

In 1927, an assassination attempt was made on the newly elected president of Mexico. The car bombing was unsuccessful. Even though Father Pro knew nothing of the attempted bombing, government officials planned to blame him. The Pro family home was invaded. Father Pro, his brother, and two others were arrested.

Father Pro and his three companions were falsely accused of attempted murder. They were put in jail and held without trial.

Father Pro was kept in prison for ten days. Along with the other prisoners, he was ridiculed and mistreated. The government officials decided to make an example of the priest and his friends. They planned to frighten Father Pro's followers by photographing his execution and making the pictures public.

Holy Friends

Father Pro was the first to die. As the cameras flashed, the priest knelt and prayed. He kissed a small cross that he always had with him. Then he stood and faced the firing squad. He stretched out his arms, like Jesus on the cross. He made the Sign of the Cross over his killers. He said, "May God have mercy on you. With all my heart I forgive my enemies." As the guns fired, he cried out, *"Viva Cristo Rey!* Long live Christ the King!"

Instead of being frightened by the photos of Father Pro's execution, his followers were inspired. Thousands upon thousands of Catholics attended Father Pro's funeral. The funeral became a public demonstration of faith. The people shouted, *"Viva Cristo Rey!"*

Pope John Paul II beatified Father Miguel Agustín Pro on September 25, 1988. His feast day is November 23.

Blessed Miguel, you, like Jesus, forgave those who put you to death. Help me to forgive, even when it's hard, anyone who has hurt or offended me.

Saint Roque González de Santa Cruz, Saint Alonso Rodríguez, and Saint Juan de Castillo

"The forest is my cathedral."
— Saint Roque

Roque González de Santa Cruz, the son of noble Spanish parents, was born in 1576 in Asunción, Paraguay. He was ordained a priest at the age of twenty-three.

Roque became very interested in the native tribes of Paraguay. His heart burned to bring the word of God to those who had never heard of Jesus. Ten years later, to prepare for this missionary work, he joined the Jesuits.

The Jesuit priests wanted to save the native tribes from the dangers of slavery. They gathered the people and brought them inland, into the remote forests. Here, they would be safer from slave traders, who kidnapped and sold people living near the cities.

Father González was one of the first descendants of Europeans to enter the deep forests of South America. There the Jesuits worked to establish missions known as "reductions." The native people who wanted to learn about and follow Jesus lived at these settlements. Father González learned to speak their language. He loved living and working among them.

For twenty years, Father González served happily in the missions. He supervised the building of churches, schools, and homes. He cared for the people when they were sick. He taught them how to farm, and how to keep cattle and sheep. On religious feast days, Father González always said Mass outside the little church. Then the whole village would celebrate with games, bonfires, dances, and music.

Father González was beloved by the native people. He lived just as they lived. He ate what they ate. In years when crops failed and there wasn't a good harvest, he suffered hunger just as they did.

In Spain, two more Jesuits prepared to join Father González. Father Alonso Rodríguez and Father Juan de Castillo came to Paraguay in 1628. They were excited about the missionary work to be done. They met with Father González and planned new mission settlements for the local tribes.

Together the three Jesuits established a mission near the Ijuhi River. It was dedicated to Our Lady's Assumption. The three Jesuits worked cheerfully through hardships, misunderstandings, and dangers.

Father Castillo was put in charge of the mission of Our Lady's Assumption. Father González and Father Rodríguez traveled even further into the forest and established the mission of All Saints. As the number of missions increased, so did attacks. Slave traders had been able to lure some of the native people away from the missions. Then they sold them into slavery. Certain tribes became very angry about these betrayals. Some even blamed the missionaries.

In 1628, Father Roque was preparing to hang a small church bell at the All Saints mission. Suddenly, he was attacked from behind. An angry tribesman killed him with a tomahawk. Father Rodríguez ran to aid his friend. He too was killed. Their bodies were thrown into the wooden chapel. Then the chapel was set on fire. The mission was destroyed.

Two days later, the same tribe attacked the mission of Our Lady's Assumption. Father Castillo, too, was seized and killed.

After the deaths of these Paraguay martyrs, the Christians living at the missions reported many signs and miracles.

In 1988, Pope John Paul II canonized Father González, Father Rodríguez, and Father Castillo. Their feast day is November 17.

Saint Roque, Saint Alonso, and Saint Juan, you loved Jesus so much that you left the safety of home to bring his Gospel to others. Help me to live and to spread the Gospel in my family and at school.

Saint Rose of Lima

1586–1617

"When we serve the poor and the sick, we serve Jesus."

In 1586, Isabel de Flores y del Oliva was the tenth child born to Spanish immigrants in Lima, Peru. Because of her pink cheeks, the family called the baby Rose. When three more children were born, Rose was a loving big sister. She also studied reading and writing, took care of the family vegetable garden, and learned to embroider linen.

Rose loved going to daily Mass with her family. She enjoyed reading about the lives of the saints. At a young age, Rose decided to dedicate her life to God. She wanted to imitate Saint Catherine of Siena. But Rose didn't know whether God was calling her to join a religious Order or to serve him while living her life at home.

One day, while Rose was tending the garden, a black and white butterfly settled on her shoulder. She took this as a sign that God wanted her to join the Third Order of Saint Dominic. Rose joined the Order and wore the black and white habit, but lived at home.

Rose worried that her beauty might endanger her loving relationship with God. She tried to hide her physical beauty, and worked instead on creating beauty within her soul. With the help of her brother, she built a little hut in the family garden. There, she lived simply, praying and singing to the Lord.

The neighbors were not used to anyone serving God in this way. Rose was often ridiculed and teased, even by some members of her family. Her parents wanted her to marry, but she refused to consider it. She wanted to live for Jesus alone. It was very hard for Rose when her parents were upset with her, but Rose always forgave them. She prayed, "Please, God, allow my sufferings to increase your love in my heart."

When her family lost all their money, Rose sewed exquisite lace. She embroidered linens with beautiful images of the different birds she had seen in her garden. She sold her handiwork at the local market. She also raised fruits, vegetables, and herbs for sale.

On the way to market, Rose often visited the sick and dying. She fed them, bathed them, and prayed with them. Rose was upset with the Spanish treatment of the native people of Peru. She protested against the unfairness of the Spanish conquerors. Some of them were dishonest and cruel, stealing from anyone they could, even injuring or killing people. Rose became known as the "mother of the poor."

After daily Mass, Rose spent hours before the Blessed Sacrament in prayer. Sometimes, she meditated quietly so that she could hear messages from God. Doctors and priests saw her at prayer and learned of her visions. They spent many hours with Rose to find out whether she truly was hearing messages from God or was just imagining them.

They discovered that God really was communicating with her. Rose became known as a saint. Word of her holiness spread throughout neighboring villages and beyond. Many came to her little garden hut to witness her faith and seek her advice.

Rose died in Lima, Peru, in 1617 at the age of thirty-one. Fifty-four years later, Pope Clement X canonized her as the first saint of the New World. Saint Rose of Lima is the patroness of the Americas. She is also known as the founder of social work in Peru. Her feast day is celebrated on August 23.

Saint Rose, through prayer and service to the poor you developed true beauty. Help God's love and beauty to grow within my heart.

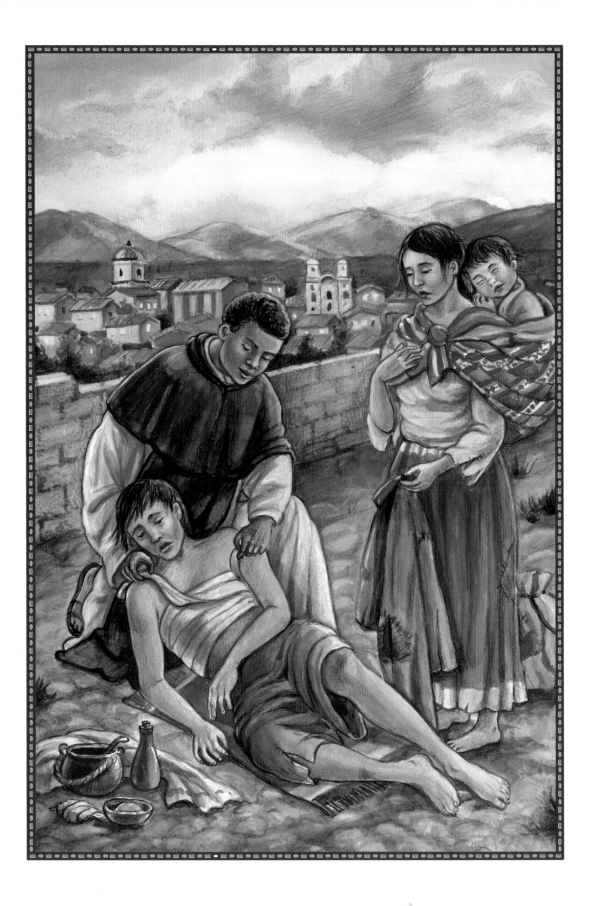

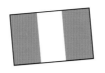

Saint Martin de Porres

1579–1639

"A torrent of tears could never wash from my soul the stain of neglect toward the homeless."

In 1579, Martin de Porres was born in Lima, Peru. His father, Juan de Porres, was Spanish. His mother, Ana Velazquez, was a free woman of African descent. In those days, a person belonging to one race was not allowed to marry someone of a different racial background. Because of this, Martin's parents could not officially marry. Juan de Porres was unhappy that Martin and his sister Juana resembled their darker-skinned mother. For several years he even rejected the children, and Señora Velazquez had to raise them on her own.

Life was not easy for the little family. People were not always kind to Martin and Juana, because they were of mixed race. The children were sometimes treated unfairly. These experiences didn't make Martin bitter or angry, though. He grew up understanding that it's important to treat everyone with respect.

As Martin and Juana got older, their father finally began to assume some responsibility for them. He sent them to school and provided financial support to their mother. Life got a little easier.

When Martin was twelve, he became an apprentice to a barber-surgeon. He learned not only to cut hair, but also to treat wounds and to prepare and administer medicine. These skills served him well when, at the age of fifteen, he entered the Dominican Order. Martin cared for the sick and dying, treating all his patients with love, no matter what their race or nationality. One day, he brought a homeless beggar to the friary infirmary, but the infirmary was already filled.

"Come," Martin invited his patient. "Rest in my bed." His superior was outraged. "We don't allow dirty people in the friary!" he exclaimed.

Martin sighed, "Forgive my error, and please instruct me, Father. I didn't know that the rule of obedience was more important than love of neighbor."

The superior grumbled, but considered Martin's gentle words. "You have within you the heart of Jesus," he finally said. "I want you, Martin, to be head of the infirmary."

Brother Martin would walk the streets of Lima calling out, "Please, rich citizens, give money to help the poor!" With the money he raised, Martin built a large orphanage for homeless children. He cared for slaves brought from Africa, tended to their sick, and taught them about Jesus. He loved animals, and treated their wounds and illnesses, too. He became known as "Martin of Charity."

Soon wonderful things started happening whenever Brother Martin was around. A dying homeless man became healthy. People without hope began to feel happiness when Brother Martin smiled at them. A Dominican friar, awaiting surgery to remove his diseased leg, found that his leg was healed after Martin came to visit him.

One time an injured man on the streets cried out, "Brother Martin, help me!" The friar suddenly appeared and tended to the man's wounds. At the same time, Brother Martin was visiting the orphanage! This special gift of bilocation, or the ability to be in two places at once, left many calling Martin a saint.

After serving the community for nearly five decades, Brother Martin de Porres fell gravely ill. He died in 1639. Along with crowds of people, government officials, a cardinal, and a bishop attended the funeral of this humble friar. Pope John XXIII canonized Martin de Porres in 1962. His feast day is November 3.

Saint Martin, you didn't allow discrimination to keep you from doing God's work. Help me to treat everyone with love and respect because we are all God's children.

Blessed Junípero Serra

1713–1784

"Come, come to receive the faith of Jesus Christ!"

Miguel José Serra was born in 1713 on the Spanish island of Mallorca. His parents sent him to a nearby Franciscan school. Miguel's teachers were impressed with his intelligence, obedience, and strong faith. He was a novice in the Franciscan Order by the age of sixteen.

While a student, Miguel was inspired by the story of Saint Francis Solano, who had been a missionary to South America. The young novice decided that, if God willed it, he too would become a missionary to the New World. In 1736, he was ordained a priest, taking the name Junípero.

Fray (Father) Junípero Serra was only about five feet tall, but his energy and ambition made him stand out in a crowd. When he was only twenty-four, he became a theology professor at a university in Palma, Spain. Twelve years later, his dream of becoming a missionary came true.

At the age of thirty-six, Fray Serra volunteered to serve in the Franciscan missions in New Spain

(California and Mexico). He left Spain and sailed across the ocean. Despite ill health from the long voyage, he insisted on walking over 200 miles from Vera Cruz to his mission in Mexico City. His strength and willpower were legendary.

For nearly fifteen years, Fray Serra served in Mexico, preaching, hearing confessions, and teaching. He loved his work in the New World. He wrote, "We have seen Indians in immense numbers. All those on the coast of the Pacific survive by plantings on various seeds, and by fishing. They fish by means of rafts or canoes, made of *tule* (bulrushes) which carry them a great way into sea. These Indians are very friendly."

In 1767, the Spanish leaders told the Jesuit priests to leave California. The government asked the Franciscan Order to take over and to establish the rights of Spain. Fray Serra, at the age of fifty-six, was chosen to do this difficult work. In spite of asthma and other physical ailments, he still had enormous energy. He founded the Mission of San Diego in 1769. In all, he established nine missions as far north as Sonoma, a 700-mile area. Eventually, there were a total of twenty-one California missions.

Fray Serra traveled between the missions by horse and by foot. Life was hard for the missionaries. At times Fray Serra and his companions were near starvation. Their faith in God gave them strength.

Fray Junípero Serra made great demands on himself, as well as on others. His desire was to convert thousands of Native Americans. God was able to reach and inspire many people through him. In all, 6,000 Native Americans were baptized.

Many people consider Fray Junípero Serra to be "the founder of California." Fray Serra played a key role in bringing Christianity to the west coast of the New World. He also assisted in planting crops, constructing buildings, scheduling ships, and planning roads. The missions produced all the colony's cattle and grain. They were important centers for trade as well as for religion.

Fray Junípero Serra made his last tour of the upper California missions in 1784. He died peacefully at Mission San Carlos on August 28, 1784. He was buried there, in the New World that he loved.

In 1987, Pope John Paul II declared Fray Junípero Serra blessed. His feast day is July 1.

Blessed Junípero, God was able to accomplish wonderful things through you. I ask God to help me bring his love and truth to all I meet.

Saint Elizabeth Ann Seton

1774–1821

"Finally, my soul is sensibly convinced of an entire surrender of itself and faculties to God."

Elizabeth Ann Bayley was born on August 28, 1774, to a wealthy family in New York. Her mother died when she was three, and her father remarried soon after. Within eight years, the Bayleys had six more children. Elizabeth was raised as an Episcopalian. She was a happy and cheerful girl, and was devoted to prayer and reading the Bible. She also loved riding horses.

When Elizabeth was nineteen, she married William Magee Seton. William was a wealthy merchant. Soon there were five children in their happy household. Life seemed perfect. Elizabeth was grateful for all her blessings. She passed her deep religious faith on to her children. But then things started to go wrong.

First Elizabeth's father, a doctor, died of yellow fever. Then her husband fell ill with tuberculosis. His business started to fail and their fortune was dwindling. "Take your husband to Italy," a doctor advised. "The climate there may improve his health."

The Setons traveled to Europe, but William died shortly after their arrival. Elizabeth was very sad and discouraged. "I think the greatest gift of this life would be to be released from the cares of the world," she wrote. But Elizabeth soon found strength through her religious faith.

While she was in Italy, Elizabeth stayed with Catholic friends. They took her to church and taught her the Rosary. Elizabeth was strongly attracted to the Catholic faith. She believed in the Real Presence of Jesus in the Blessed Sacrament. She was devoted to the Blessed Mother. She also began to understand that the Catholic Church is directly traced back to Christ and his apostles.

When Elizabeth returned to New York, she found that all her money was gone. She had to support herself and her five children, and she decided to become a teacher. Elizabeth studied more about the Catholic faith and became a Catholic at the age of thirty. Her Protestant family and friends were not happy. They refused to accept Elizabeth or her children as family any more.

Father Dubourg, a priest friend, asked Elizabeth to move to Baltimore, Maryland, to open a Catholic school for girls. Elizabeth and her children traveled there together. Maryland was the first state in the United States to allow Catholics to freely practice their faith. Elizabeth and her children felt at home there.

In Baltimore, Elizabeth established a school for girls, and she continued to raise her family. Eventually, she and five other women founded a religious Congregation. It was the first American religious community for women. They called it the Sisters of Charity of Saint Joseph. Elizabeth became the mother superior.

Mother Seton led her community for twelve years. The Sisters of Charity continued to grow. They brought education to the poor and helped establish the parochial school system in the United States. Elizabeth had received an excellent education as a young girl. She taught classes and even wrote many of the text-books herself.

Mother Elizabeth Seton worked tirelessly despite the long and painful illness of tuberculosis. She remained close to her children. Sadly, two of her daughters died at young ages. A son died at the age of twenty-six.

Mother Elizabeth Ann Seton was only forty-six when she died of tuberculosis. She was the first American-born citizen to be beatified and canonized. Pope Paul VI declared her a saint on September 14, 1975. Her feast day is January 4.

Saint Elizabeth Ann, you showed us how by inner strength we can grow in faith and hope through life's trials. Help me to cope with life's problems and use them to grow and change for the better.

Saint Rose Philippine Duchesne

1769–1852

"God does not require great achievements,
but a heart that holds back nothing for self."

Rose Philippine Duchesne was born to a wealthy family in France in 1769. She was named after Saint Rose and Saint Philip the apostle. Like Saint Rose, she possessed strong faith and a desire to help others. Like Saint Philip, she wanted to bring the Good News of Jesus Christ to those who did not know him. Her favorite subject in school was history. Rose also became very interested in stories of Native Americans. She dreamed of becoming a missionary in the New World.

Rose was a faithful Catholic during the French Revolution. During the Revolution, many Catholics were killed or imprisoned for their faith. Because they feared for her safety, her parents didn't want her to become a sister. In time, though, Rose convinced them of her calling. When she was seventeen, they allowed her to enter the Visitation convent.

Soon after she entered, the convent was forced to close because of the Revolution. Rose returned to her home, but she was still determined to serve Jesus and the Church. She organized a group of women to work with the poor and sick. She also risked her life to hide priests from the revolutionaries.

Ten years later, when the Reign of Terror finally ended, Rose entered the Society of the Sacred Heart. She studied there and finally took her vows. She became Sister Rose Philippine. Her Congregation was dedicated to prayer and service work in France. Still, Sister Rose knew that someday God would call her to serve the people of the New World.

In 1818, when Sister Rose was fifty years old, her dream finally came true. The bishop asked for teachers to travel to the Louisiana Territory in the United States. Sister Rose and four other sisters sailed to the New World to establish their Congregation. They settled in Missouri. Sister Rose became the superior.

The first ten years in the United States were very hard. Bitter cold, terrible heat, diseases, hunger, forest fires, and shortages of drinking water were major problems. Mother Duchesne was determined and full of enthusiasm. In Missouri, she and her Congregation opened the first free school west of the Mississippi River for Catholic and non-Catholic children. They also founded an orphanage, a free parish school, and a boarding school. Many young women wanted to join the Congregation, and they opened more convents.

As her Congregation grew, Mother Duchesne continued to travel and work. She became ill with yellow fever and nearly died. Finally, when she was seventy years old, she went to work with Native Americans in the north-western United States. Although she was in frail health, her superiors knew Mother Duchesne still wanted to serve the Native American people.

Mother Duchesne left St. Louis and made the four-day journey to Sugar Creek, Kansas. At the settlement, 700 Potawatomi tribal members greeted her arrival.

Mother Duchesne found great joy in opening a new school at the settlement and teaching the children. Her beloved Potawatomi children named her *Quah-kah-ka-num-ad,* "Woman-who-prays-always." Mother Duchesne served for thirty-four years in the United States. She died at the age of eighty-three. Pope John Paul II canonized her on July 3, 1988. Her feast day is November 18.

Saint Rose Philippine, you served God patiently and waited nearly your entire life to see your childhood dreams fulfilled. Help me to trust in God's will for me as I grow.

Blessed Theodore Guérin

1798–1856

"With Jesus, what shall we have to fear?"

Anne-Thérèse Guérin was born in Etables-sur-Mer, France, in 1798. At the age of ten, she received her First Communion. That day, she told her parish priest that someday she would dedicate herself to God and God's work.

When Anne was fifteen, her father was killed. She took care of her mother and younger sister for several years. In 1823, she entered the convent of the Sisters of Providence. These sisters served as teachers and cared for the sick. While still a novice, Anne became ill. She would suffer from poor health for the rest of her life.

When Anne took her vows, she chose Sister Theodore as her religious name. For eighteen years she served as a teacher in schools and parishes in France. She also visited and helped poor people who were sick.

In 1840, missionaries were badly needed in the United States. When her bishop asked for sisters to volunteer to teach there, Sister Theodore remained silent. She had no dreams of becoming a missionary!

She didn't really want to leave the country and home that she so dearly loved. Then she learned that she would indeed be needed to teach in the United States. She honored her vow of obedience, and agreed to go.

Sister Theodore and five other sisters left France for a hazardous three-month voyage to the United States. Their ship was nearly destroyed by hurricanes and severe storms. Sister Theodore wrote in her diary, "Passing the night in the bottom of the vessel, hearing continually the dreadful creaking, makes one fear that the ship will split open." After another storm, she wrote, "Nothing was heard on board but cries and prayers."

After finally landing in New York, Sister Theodore and her companions traveled by stagecoach, train, steamboat, and canal boat to Indiana. They journeyed through forests and across dangerous rivers. Sister Theodore wrote, "We continued through the thick woods until suddenly, Father Buteux stopped the carriage and said, 'Come down, Sisters, we have arrived.' What an astonishment to find ourselves in the midst of forest, no village, not even a house in sight!"

Down a ravine was their new home, Saint Mary of the Woods. Four new members waited for them. Sister Theodore was put in charge and became "Mother Theodore."

While at Saint Mary of the Woods, Mother Theodore organized and established a boarding school for girls. Soon there were ten schools for girls and two orphanages. Together with her sisters, Mother Theodore met the challenges of life in this wild frontier. They often lacked food and other basic necessities. At that time, many people were also suspicious and fearful of Catholics, especially Catholic sisters. This made things even harder for the little community.

Mother Theodore and her sisters lived under constant threats to their safety. But Mother Theodore's faith was strong. "With Jesus, what shall we have to fear?" she said. The sisters worked hard. Their community continued to grow.

Eventually, Mother Theodore served a busy community of sixty sisters, 1,200 students, and ten parish schools. Her health weakened until her death at the age of fifty-seven. Pope John Paul II beatified Mother Theodore Guérin on October 25, 1998. Her feast day is May 14.

Blessed Theodore, you were able to honor your vow of obedience when God called you. When life is challenging, help me to make good decisions, just as you did.

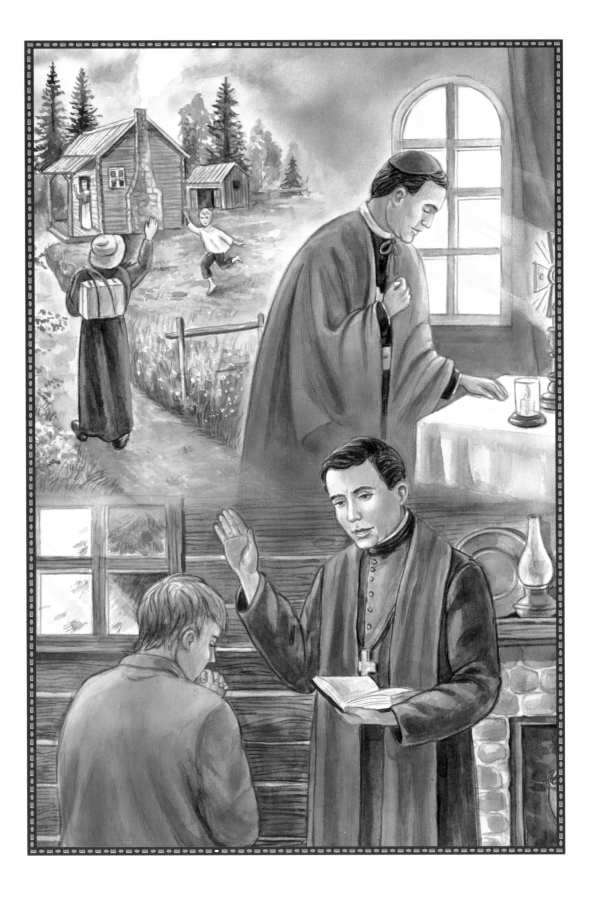

Saint John Neumann

1811–1860

"...Every man has the right to an education...this education should pave the way to brotherly love so that genuine unity and peace on earth prevail."

John Neumann was born in Bohemia (now called the Czech Republic), in 1811. He was the third of six children. John was a small child, and barely reached five feet tall even as an adult. He was intelligent and worked hard at school. While he was studying to become a priest, he dreamed of one day going as a missionary to Canada or the United States. He studied English and French along with other courses.

But when John graduated at the top of his class, the bishop refused to ordain him! There were already many priests in Bohemia, and no money available to support more. Catholic priests were urgently needed in the United States, however. John decided to travel there to become a priest.

John was ordained in Buffalo, New York. The Catholic community there was very happy to welcome him. Father John asked if he could serve as a parish priest out in the countryside. He built himself a small log cabin. Even the church in his town was built with logs! Many of his parishioners were farmers who lived very far apart. Sometimes he walked thirty miles to say Mass.

Father John worked hard to serve his people, so hard that he became ill. During his recovery, he joined the Redemptorist Congregation. He became the first person of this Congregation to make his vows in the United States.

Father John Neumann served in New York, Maryland, Virginia, and Ohio. He was very popular among new immigrants. He could speak twelve different languages! German-speaking people felt especially close to Father Neumann. He wrote two catechisms in German. He founded the first national parish for Italians in the United States. Father John wanted to improve life for all poor immigrants.

Father John became well known for his holiness, great preaching, and writings. In 1852, he was named the fourth bishop of Philadelphia. Bishop Neumann also became known for his leadership skills and for organizing Philadelphia's Catholic school system. In less than three years, the number of children in Catholic schools grew from 500 to 9,000. He cared deeply about education.

But Bishop Neumann did not want new immigrants to forget where they came from. He wanted them to remember and share their cultures. He believed that this was an important part of true education.

In five years, Bishop John Neumann saw fifty churches built in his diocese. He began building a cathedral. He opened almost 100 schools, and founded a seminary. He also began a new Congregation of Franciscan Sisters.

Even after all these successes, Bishop Neumann remained humble. When he saw a beggar sleeping under a pile of newspapers in the park, he said, "There but by the grace of God go I." Church leaders in Rome asked if he wished to continue as bishop of Philadelphia or be given an easier job. Bishop Neumann answered, "I desire nothing but to fulfill the wish of the Holy Father, whatever it may be."

Bishop Neumann never regained his full health. The stressful pace of his work began to take its toll. Bishop John Neumann died suddenly from a stroke when he was just forty-eight years old.

Pope Paul VI canonized John Neumann on June 19, 1977. He is the first American bishop to be named a saint. His feast day is January 5.

Saint John, you respected people from many different cultures and countries. Help me to be accepting and tolerant of people who are different than me.

Blessed Francis Xavier Seelos

1819–1867

*"I love the work of the missions more than all other labors....
Someday, I will become a second Francis Xavier."*

Francis Seelos was born in 1819 in Germany, the sixth of nine children. His deeply religious parents named him after Saint Francis Xavier. The Seelos family read Scripture and the lives of saints together every night after dinner. Francis became an altar server at an early age. Later he entered the seminary to become a parish priest. One night, a vision changed his plans forever.

The next morning Francis told his brother, "Last night the Blessed Mother appeared to me. I want to become a missionary." He applied to the superior of the Redemptorist Congregation in the United States. He was quickly accepted.

Francis and three other students arrived in New York and traveled to Baltimore. He was ordained a year later and remained in Baltimore for eight months. Then he was sent to Pittsburgh to assist Father John Neumann. Father Neumann (who later became Saint John Neumann) had a profound influence on young

Father Seelos. Father Seelos said, "In every respect, Pastor Neumann was a remarkable father to me. His examples of great humility and patience are vivid in my memory." Father Seelos was soon transferred to a large parish and school, where he served as pastor and religious superior.

Father Seelos performed the duties of priesthood with great energy. He became known for his preaching in German, French, and English. He would act out Scripture stories, including imaginary conversations with Jesus, his apostles, and other characters in the Bible. Sometimes his sermons were very funny, which was unusual for that time.

In celebrating the sacrament of Reconciliation, Father Seelos listened to everyone with great kindness. Because of his gentle understanding, people would wait for hours in line for him to hear their confessions. The pews were packed for his services. People came to see him at all hours of the day and night. In fact, he often slept in his clothes so he would be ready if his doorbell rang.

One cold night he went out to celebrate the Anointing of the Sick with a dying person. On his way back to the rectory, he saw a homeless man wearing rags on his feet. Father Seelos took off his own boots and gave them to the man. He walked home in his stocking feet. Whenever people were sick, he stayed by their bedsides and prayed. Father Seelos was even known to gather the laundry at a sick person's bedside and to wash and return it himself!

Father Seelos worked very hard all the time. When the Civil War began, he and his students moved to Annapolis, Maryland. Later, he traveled from parish to parish preaching and giving retreats. He was a missionary in Missouri, Illinois, Wisconsin, Ohio, Pennsylvania, New York, New Jersey, Connecticut, and Rhode Island. He wrote to his sister, "I love the work of the missions more than anything else. It is the work in the vineyard of the Lord."

In 1866, on his way to New Orleans, Father Seelos had a vision that he would die soon. The following year, there was a terrible outbreak of yellow fever. This beloved pastor died of the fever at the age of forty-eight. Pope John Paul II beatified Francis Xavier Seelos in the year 2000. His feast day is October 4.

Blessed Francis Xavier, you used faith, words, and actions to spread God's love throughout the United States. Help me to serve God and my neighbor with love.

Blessed Damien Joseph de Veuster

1840–1889

"I make myself a leper with the lepers,
to gain all for Jesus Christ."

Joseph de Veuster was born in Tremeloo, Belgium, on January 3, 1840. When he was younger, he had a very short temper. He was also known at his school as a bit of a problem! Fortunately, as he grew older, Joseph learned to use his energy in better ways.

While he was at college, Joseph realized that God was calling him to give himself totally in service of others. He joined the Congregation of the Sacred Hearts of Jesus and Mary, and became Brother Damien. He entered the seminary and began to study for the priesthood.

Brother Damien's brother, who was already ordained, was going to be a missionary on the islands of Hawaii. Right before he was supposed to leave, he became ill. The doctors would not allow him to travel. Even though Brother Damien was not yet ordained a priest, he asked to travel to Hawaii in his brother's place.

It took over four months to sail to the islands. The same year that he arrived, Brother Damien completed his studies and was ordained. Father Damien's first ministry was on the Big Island of Hawaii.

His very first task was to help the 350 Catholics build a new church. The Hawaiians were friendly and willing to share their lives with Father Damien. Together on the Big Island, they survived volcano eruptions, a tidal wave that wiped out many homes and the church, and damaging hurricanes.

Leprosy, a contagious disease that had been brought to the islands by foreigners, was a terrible problem. It disfigured its victims, leaving sores all over the body and causing deformities. Today it is called Hansen's disease, and it can be treated and cured. At that time, though, there was no cure for leprosy.

The Board of Health tried to halt the disease by requiring that anyone with leprosy live apart from everyone else. They decided that the small island of Molokai would be the isolated area for people with leprosy to live. Ten years after Father Damien arrived at the Hawaiian Islands, he volunteered to minister to the dying lepers on Molokai.

At first, being with the lepers was upsetting to Father Damien. There were unpleasant smells. The lepers coughed constantly. But his love was very deep, and he was strong and determined. He refused to leave. "I will do anything to help these poor people," he said.

Father Damien became a loving father to all the people of Molokai. He built houses and tended to the sick. He laid a pipeline to bring water to the settlement. He buried the dead. The King and Queen of Hawaii sent supplies and help when he asked. They honored Father Damien for all his hard work.

Fifteen years after his arrival at the leper colony, Father Damien also contracted leprosy. He had open sores on his skin, and his face was badly disfigured. He lost all of his fingers except the ones that held the holy Host when he celebrated Mass. Father Damien's eyes were always inflamed and sore. It was hard for him to breathe.

After tenderly helping over 1,000 people with leprosy, Father Damien died of the disease on Palm Sunday at the age of forty-nine. He was buried on Molokai, but later his body was returned to Belgium.

Pope John Paul II beatified Damien Joseph de Veuster on June 4, 1995. His feast day is April 15.

Blessed Damien, you used your stubbornness and fierce loyalty to serve the outcasts of society. I want to use my gifts for the good of others, too.

Saint Frances Xavier Cabrini

1850–1917

"Of these schools, hospitals, orphanages...I have not done it...God has done it all, and I have merely looked on."

Saint Frances Xavier Cabrini was one of the most active saints in the Americas. She was born in Italy, the youngest of thirteen children. As a child, Frances dreamed of becoming a missionary in China. When she turned eighteen, she became a teacher. She loved working with children.

At twenty-two she first tried to enter a religious Congregation. She was turned down due to her poor health. She later tried another religious community and was turned down again. Finally, she became a Third Order (Secular) Franciscan and taught poor children and orphans.

A visiting priest noticed Frances's good work with the orphans. "I know you want to become a sister," he said. "There are six other women here who feel the same. With your companions, you can begin a Congregation of your own." The bishop approved the new Congregation, called the Missionary Sisters of the

Sacred Heart of Jesus. Sister Frances was named the superior. She became known as Mother Cabrini.

After the Missionary Sisters opened three new convents, the Vatican allowed them to open two more convents in Rome as well as a free school and a children's home. One day, in a private meeting with Pope Leo XIII, Mother Cabrini said, "I wish to become a missionary to China." The pope listened, but shook his head. "Not to the East, but to the West," he said. "We need missionaries in America to assist with the Italian immigrants."

In March of 1889, Mother Cabrini and six companion sisters sailed to New York. Their welcome by the local bishop was far from friendly. "You might as well board the next ship back to Italy," he said. "There is no suitable place for you here." But Mother Cabrini gently refused. "The Holy Father has sent us, and we will stay!" Within a few weeks, she found a home for her sisters and even raised funds to open an orphanage.

Mother Cabrini's travels were not over. Many times she was needed back in Italy on business. In the meantime, her Congregation grew both in Italy and in the United States. Mother Cabrini established a community of sisters in New Orleans. Later, she took fourteen of her sisters to Nicaragua and Panama, in Central America. Then her travels took her to South America. She opened convents and orphanages in Argentina and Brazil. In her lifetime, she founded sixty-seven schools, hospitals, orphanages, and missions.

Mother Cabrini was a very wise woman. Once, sellers of property in Chicago tried to cheat her out of land on which a hospital was to be built. Mother Cabrini went and measured the land herself. After uncovering the dishonesty, she fired the builders. Then she personally supervised the building of the hospital.

While in South America, Mother Cabrini became ill with malaria. Even though she was often sick, she continued her busy pace. "When I am working, I am well. I fall sick the instant I stop working," she said.

Mother Cabrini became an American citizen while she was working in Seattle. As her health failed, she settled with her sisters in Chicago. It was there that she died at the age of sixty-seven. Pope Pius XII canonized Mother Frances Xavier Cabrini in 1946. Her feast day is November 13.

Saint Frances, you didn't allow rejection to stop you from moving forward and serving God in the world. Help me to overcome obstacles to doing good.

Saint Katharine Drexel

1858–1955

"There is a void in my heart that only God can fill."

There is an old saying that money is the root of all evil. This saying could never be applied to Katharine Drexel. Katharine inherited over seven million dollars from her family. She used her money in generous, loving ways. In this case, money became a means of spreading goodness on earth.

Katharine Drexel was born in Philadelphia, Pennsylvania, the second daughter in a very wealthy family. Her mother died when Katharine was only five weeks old. Two years later, her father married again. Soon, the Drexels were blessed with another daughter.

Katharine's stepmother loved her stepdaughters. The three Drexel girls received the finest educations. The Drexels were also faithful Catholics. They wanted to serve the poor members of Philadelphia society. Katharine and her family opened their home to feed, clothe, and educate the poor and homeless in Philadelphia.

"What you are doing for the poor in society is beautiful," the bishop said to Katharine one day. "Serving the poor makes me feel satisfied," she answered. "I believe that God wants me to serve others as a religious sister." The bishop nodded. "Think, pray, and wait," he advised. "God will let you know his will."

Katharine had to put her call to religious life on hold when her beloved stepmother developed cancer. Katharine took care of her for the last three years of her life. After her death, Katharine's father died of a sudden heart attack. The Drexel sisters left for Europe to grieve and to plan their futures.

While she was in Rome, Katharine prayed. She waited for God's direction. Then she had a special meeting with Pope Leo XIII. "Could you send more missionaries to help Native Americans and African Americans?" she asked. But Pope Leo just smiled and answered, "Why don't *you* become their missionary?"

Within four years Katharine and her sisters had contributed money to build and support thirteen mission schools in the western states of America. They donated nearly two million dollars to fund Native American education. But this was not enough for Katharine! She told her bishop, "I wish to give the remainder of my life to helping Native Americans and African Americans."

Katharine entered the Sisters of Mercy in 1889. Soon afterward, she started a new Congregation, the Sisters of the Blessed Sacrament. She was known as Mother Mary Katharine. For the next forty years, Mother Katharine followed her vow to be mother and servant of the poor. She worked very hard to teach children skills to help them lift themselves out of poverty. She also worked to bring them closer to Jesus in the Eucharist.

Mother Katharine had problems with people who didn't want schools for African Americans or Native Americans in their neighborhoods. Some schools were burned. Others were damaged. But nothing would keep Mother Katharine from her work. She knew that love was stronger than hatred.

Mother Katharine Drexel had a heart attack at the age of seventy-seven. From then on, she devoted herself to constant prayer. She died twenty years later, at the age of ninety-seven. At the time of her death, Mother Katharine had used all her inheritance to establish 145 Catholic missions, 12 schools for Native Americans, and 50 schools for African Americans.

Pope John Paul II canonized her on October 1, 2000. Her feast day is celebrated on March 3.

Saint Katharine, you gave everything back to God out of love—your life, your wealth, and all you owned. Help me to be as generous and unselfish as you were.

Glossary

Apprentice—a person who serves another for a period of time in order to learn an art or trade.

Apparition—someone or something that appears and can be seen by others.

Archbishop—a **bishop** who leads the Catholic Church in a large **diocese,** known as an archdiocese.

Basilica—a large church of special importance that is patterned after a type of ancient Roman building.

Beatification—the ceremony in which the pope recognizes that a deceased person lived a life of Gospel holiness in a heroic way. In most cases, a proven **miracle** obtained through the holy person's prayers to God is also required. Beatification is the second step toward declaring someone a saint. A person who is beatified is given the title Blessed.

Bishop—a priest who has received the fullness of the Sacrament of Holy Orders, which makes him a successor of the Apostles. A bishop leads the Catholic Church in a specific area called a **diocese.**

Blessed Sacrament—another name for the Holy Eucharist, the real Body and Blood of the risen Jesus present under the appearances of bread and wine at Mass. Blessed Sacrament is the name especially used to refer to the Holy Eucharist kept, in the form of consecrated hosts, in the tabernacle.

Brother—a male religious who makes vows of poverty, chastity, and obedience, and lives in community.

Canonization—the ceremony in which the pope officially declares that a person is a **saint** in heaven. To canonize someone is to recognize that he or she has lived a life of heroic virtue, is worthy of imitation, and can intercede for others. Like **beatification,** canonization requires a miracle resulting from the holy person's **intercession.**

Congregation (religious)—a community of men or women who live together and follow a Rule approved by the Church, and make vows of poverty, chastity, and obedience to God. The members of a Congregation share a life of prayer and carry out special works of service for the good of God's people.

Consecrated—that which has been made or declared sacred.

Convert—to turn, especially from nonbelief to faith.

Diocese—a territory made up of parishes placed by the pope under the care of a bishop.

Embroidery—the art of making decorative designs with needlework.

Episcopalian—a member of the Episcopal Church, which traces its origin to the Church of England established by King Henry VIII.

Excommunicated—the word "excommunicate" means "to exclude from a community." A person is excommunicated from the Catholic Church only for a very serious reason. He or she is not allowed to receive the sacraments, especially the Holy Eucharist.

Feast day—a day set aside to honor the life of a saint. The feast day is almost always the date of the saint's death since it is regarded as the beginning of the saint's new life in heaven.

First Nations' peoples—Tribal groups of people native to Canada.

Friar—a word meaning "brother." This is the name given to male members of certain religious Orders, such as the Franciscans and Dominicans. These brothers live in a house called a friary.

Habit—distinctive clothing worn by members of a religious Order or Congregation.

Holy Land—a name given to the area in the Middle East where Jesus lived, died, and rose from the dead.

Immigrants—those who come to a country to live and work.

Infirmary—a place where the sick are cared for.

Intercession—a request in favor of another person. The Blessed Mother, the angels, saints in heaven, souls in purgatory, and the faithful on earth intercede for mankind by their goodness and prayers.

Malaria—a disease that is spread by mosquitoes, which results in periodic attacks of chills and fevers. Today malaria can be prevented.

Martyr—a person who allows himself or herself to be killed rather than deny the faith.

Ministry—serving God by serving other people.

Miracle—a wonderful happening that goes beyond the powers of nature and is produced by God to teach us some truth or to testify to the holiness of a person.

Missionary—a person who is sent by the Church to bring the Gospel to people in a given place or region.

Monastery—the place where monks or nuns live as a community, dedicating themselves to a life of prayer.

Mother house—the main building and headquarters of a religious community.

Native Americans— Tribal groups of people native to the United States.

Nun—a woman who is a member of a cloistered religious Order dedicated to a hidden life of prayer, and who has taken vows of poverty, chastity, and obedience.

Order (religious)—a community of men or women who live together and make solemn vows of chastity, poverty, and obedience to God. The most important work of members of religious Orders is prayer.

Ordination—the ceremony in which a man receives the sacrament of Holy Orders. A man may be ordained a deacon, a priest, or a bishop.

Patron saint—a saint prayed to as a special protector or intercessor in relation to an individual, place, occupation, or a particular problem.

Pastor—a priest appointed by a bishop to serve a parish.

Persecution—the effort by people or by governments to stop members of a religion from practicing their faith.

Pilgrimage—a journey made to a holy place by pilgrims, people who want to pray and to feel closer to God.

Pneumonia—A lung disease caused by infection. Today pneumonia can be treated and cured.

Prioress—the superior of a house of a religious Order for women. The superior of a house of a religious Order for men is a prior.

Retreat—a period of withdrawing from the world and everyday activities to spend time in prayer, reflection, and other spiritual activities.

Sacrament—an outward sign instituted by Jesus to give grace. The Seven Sacraments are: Baptism, Confirmation, Eucharist, Reconciliation, Anointing of the Sick, Holy Orders, and Matrimony.

Seminary—a school where men are educated and trained for the priesthood.

Shrine—a holy place where people come to honor Jesus, Mary, or one of the saints.

Sister—a woman who has taken vows as a member of a religious Congregation.

Smallpox—A serious disease caused by a virus. Today smallpox can be prevented.

Sodality—a religious group whose members come together to deepen their prayer life and perform works of charity.

Superior—the title given to the person who governs and serves a religious community.

Theology—the study of God and his relations with the created universe.

Third Orders—Associations of the faithful established by religious Orders. If secular, they are laypersons, or tertiaries. If regular, they are religious, who are bound by vows and who live in community.

Tuberculosis—a disease that affects the lungs. Today tuberculosis is treatable and curable.

Typhus—a serious disease that causes high fever. Today typhus is rare in developed countries.

Vatican—the central headquarters, in Rome, Italy, of the Roman Catholic Church and the pope.

Vocation—a call from God to a certain lifestyle. A person may have a vocation to the married life, the priesthood, the religious life, or the single life. Everyone has a vocation to be holy.

Vow—an important promise freely made to God. The most common vows today are those of poverty, chastity, and obedience made by members of religious communities.

Yellow fever—a serious disease usually found in warm regions of the world and spread by the yellow-fever mosquito.

Index

Diana M. Amadeo, a member of the Secular Franciscan Order, is a former registered nurse as well as a wife and mother. Her essays and short stories have appeared in many publications and anthologies. She is the author of two children's books, *My Baby Sister Is a Preemie: Helping Kids Heal* (Zonderkidz, 2005), *There's a Little Bit of Me in Jamey* (Albert Whitman & Company, 1989), and a novel, *The Scarlet Tanager* (Aegina Press, 1995). Diana lives in New Hampshire.

Irina Lombardo was born and raised in the Udmurt Republic of Russia. She received a formal education in graphic arts at the Udmurt State University in Izhevsk and worked as a graphic designer for several years before moving to the United States. Irina currently works as a freelance artist from her studio in Chino Hills, California. Her art can be viewed at www.lombardoart.com.

Augusta Curreli was an artist, wife, and mother living in Italy. She illustrated over fifty children's books, including *My Bible: The Story of God's Love* (Pauline Books & Media, 2004). After beginning preliminary work on a number of illustrations for *Holy Friends,* Augusta passed away following a valiant nine-year battle with cancer. Irina Lombardo was able to use the inspiration of Augusta's sketches to produce the beautiful original artwork in this book.

Pauline
BOOKS & MEDIA

The Daughters of St. Paul operate book and media centers at the following addresses. Visit, call or write the one nearest you today, or find us on the World Wide Web, www.pauline.org

CALIFORNIA

3908 Sepulveda Blvd, Culver City, CA 90230 310-397-8676

5945 Balboa Avenue, San Diego, CA 92111 858-565-9181

46 Geary Street, San Francisco, CA 94108 415-781-5180

FLORIDA

145 S.W. 107th Avenue, Miami, FL 33174 305-559-6715

HAWAII

1143 Bishop Street, Honolulu, HI 96813 808-521-2731

Neighbor Islands call: 866-521-2731

ILLINOIS

172 North Michigan Avenue, Chicago, IL 60601 312-346-4228

LOUISIANA

4403 Veterans Memorial Blvd, Metairie, LA 70006 504-887-7631

MASSACHUSETTS

885 Providence Hwy, Dedham, MA 02026 781-326-5385

MISSOURI

9804 Watson Road, St. Louis, MO 63126 314-965-3512

NEW JERSEY

561 U.S. Route 1, Wick Plaza, Edison, NJ 08817 732-572-1200

NEW YORK

150 East 52nd Street, New York, NY 10022 212-754-1110

78 Fort Place, Staten Island, NY 10301 718-447-5071

PENNSYLVANIA

9171-A Roosevelt Blvd, Philadelphia, PA 19114 215-676-9494

SOUTH CAROLINA

243 King Street, Charleston, SC 29401 843-577-0175

TENNESSEE

4811 Poplar Avenue, Memphis, TN 38117 901-761-2987

TEXAS

114 Main Plaza, San Antonio, TX 78205 210-224-8101

VIRGINIA

1025 King Street, Alexandria, VA 22314 703-549-3806

CANADA

3022 Dufferin Street, Toronto, ON M6B 3T5 416-781-9131

¡También somos su fuente para libros, videos y música en español!

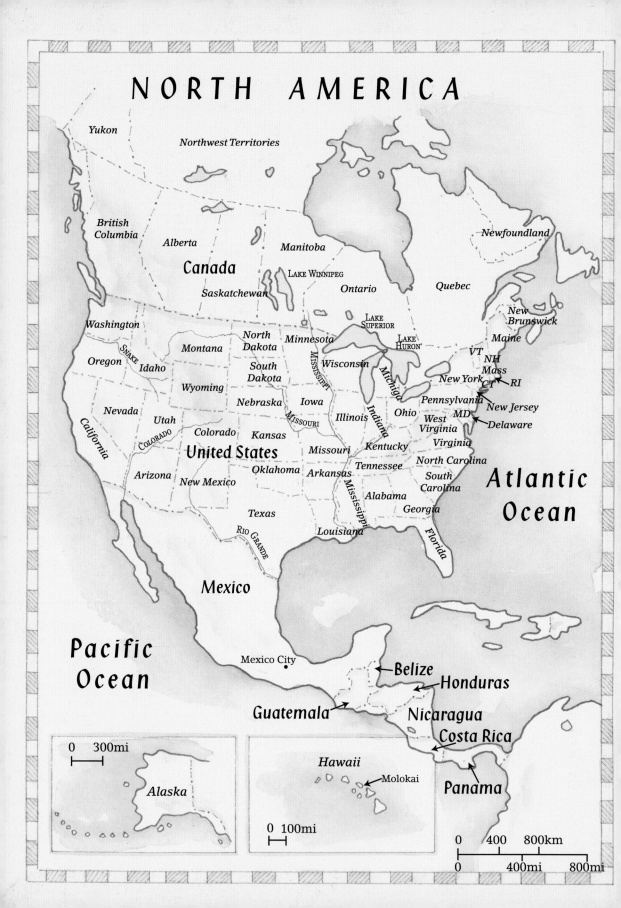